Governing From the Skies

Governing From the Skies

A Global History
of Aerial Bombing

THOMAS HIPPLER

Translated by David Fernbach

VERSO
London • New York

For Étienne Balibar

Published with the support of the Triangle research unit
(UMR 5206 of the CNRS) and of Sciences Po Lyon

The translation of this book was supported by
the Centre national du livre (CNL)

This English-language edition published by Verso 2017
Originally published as *Le gouvernement du ciel:
Histoire globale des bombardements aériens*
© Les Prairies Ordinaires 2014
Translation © David Fernbach 2017

1 3 5 7 9 10 8 6 4 2

Verso
UK: 6 Meard Street, London W1F 0EG
US: 20 Jay Street, Suite 1010, Brooklyn, NY 11201
versobooks.com

Verso is the imprint of New Left Books

ISBN-13: 978-1-78478-595-6
ISBN-13: 978-1-78478-598-7 (US EBK)
ISBN-13: 978-1-78478-597-0 (UK EBK)

British Library Cataloguing in Publication Data
A catalogue record for this book is available from the British Library

Library of Congress Cataloging-in-Publication Data

Names: Hippler, Thomas, 1972– author. | Fernbach, David, translator.
Title: Governing from the skies : a global history of
aerial bombing / Thomas
  Hippler ; translated by David Fernbach.
Other titles: Gouvernement du ciel. English
Description: New York : Verso, [2017]
Identifiers: LCCN 2016033495 (print) | LCCN
2016033523 (ebook) | ISBN
  9781784785956 (hbk. : alk. paper) | ISBN
9781784785987 ()
Subjects: LCSH: Bombing, Aerial – History.
Classification: LCC UG630 .H58613 2017 (print) |
LCC UG630 (ebook) | DDC
  358.4/2409 – dc23
LC record available at https://lccn.loc.gov/2016033495

Typeset in Sabon by MJ&N Gavan, Truro, Cornwall
Printed in the UK by CPI Group (UK) Ltd, Croydon
CR0 4YY

Contents

Acknowledgements

My thanks first of all to Nicolas Vieillescazes, not only for his support and encouragement throughout the writing of this book, but above all for the impeccable editorial work he contributed. Whatever people may say, publishing houses do still have editors! Several people have made it possible for this book to be born, each in their own way, and at different stages and moments. I particularly have to thank Jérémie Barthas for materialism in theory; Adila Benedjai-Zou for soft drinks and Sundays; Axel Berger for table tennis and revolution; Antje Bonhage for Berlin; Chiara Bottici for the radical Enlightenment; Aurélie Blanchard for art, architecture, and whisky sour; Sebastian Budgen for a mine of information; Benoît Challand for New York; Grégoire Chamayou for 'patterns of life'; Xavier Chatel for world politics and good meals; Antony Dabila for strategy; Thomas Deltombe for weapons; François Dumasy for Rome; Alexander Gumz for poetry; Isik Gurleyen for international relations theory and Turkey; Wolfgang Hardtwig for all his advice and support; Klaus, Petra, Annika, and Benjamin Hippler for their unfailing support; Vincent Jacques for overcoding and axiomatics; Oliver Janz for the invitation; Sara Jassim for graphic design; Razmig Keucheyan for his support and discussions on internationalism; Dieter Langewiesche for his criticism; Anne Lepoittevin for the razor and the *latitanza*; Chantal Malambri for Situationism; Nicola Marcucci for the title and for Berlin nights; Élise Marrou for philosophy and the Loire; Sarah Mazouz for intersectionality; Aïcha Messina for Chile; Pino Messina for Umbria; Roberto Nigro for many things over many years; Vannina Olivesi for dance and sushi; Germinal Pinalie for a volcano of ideas; Hélène Quiniou for the art of formulation; Mathieu Rigouste for the arms industry; Kahena Sanaâ for the pauses; Delphine Simon for theatre, wine, and all the good moments spent during the writing of this book; Arnault Skornicki for the social history of political ideas; Jörg Stickan for beer and literature; Hew Strachan for the First World War; Bo Strath for his kindness and benevolence; Savina Tarsitano for Calabria; Spiros Tegos for Athens; Julien Théry for his evenings; Benno Teschke for geopolitics; Chloé Thomas for translation and rock'n'roll; Miloš Vec for peace; Jérôme Vidal for friendship; Julien Vincent for technophilia; and Caterina Zanfi for the philosophy of war. My warmest gratitude here to them all.

Prologue

Tripoli, 1 November 1911. 'I decided that today I would try to drop bombs from the aeroplane. No one had ever tried such a thing, and if I succeed I shall be happy to have been the first,' Lieutenant Giulio Gavotti wrote in a letter to his father. The engineer from Genoa had obtained his pilot's wings just at the time that the Italian government decided to embark on the conquest of a colonial empire in Libya. Gavotti's record to date was limited to an unauthorized flight above the Vatican, which led to his detention for a few days, and to second place in a race between Bologna and Venice. But in late September 1911 things began to hot up in Libya: the Sublime Porte had refused to cede Tripoli and Italy declared war on the Ottoman Empire. Less than a week later, the city fell into the hands of the Italians. As a member of a small 'airmen's flotilla', Gavotti was posted to Africa a few days after his twenty-ninth birthday.

At dawn on 1 November, Gavotti took off in his plane and headed for the Mediterranean. He had no specific mission order, but he did have a definite idea. He made a wide turn above the sea before heading for the small oasis of Aïn Zara, some fifteen kilometres south-east of Tripoli, where he had noticed a troop of Arab fighters on an earlier reconnaissance flight:

> I held the joystick with one hand, and with the other I untied the cord that held the cover of the box. I took a bomb from the box, which I placed on my knees. Transferring the joystick to my other hand, with the free one I removed a

detonator from the small box. I put it in my mouth. I closed the box, placed the detonator in the bomb and looked down. I was ready. I was about one kilometre from the oasis.

The Ottoman army, caught unawares by the Italian aggression, met with considerable difficulties. So much so that Fethi Bey, the Ottoman military commander of the Tripoli region, decided to withdraw his troops and call on indigenous units to use guerrilla tactics. Gavotti's task in Libya was to undertake strategic reconnaissance missions and keep the general staff informed of the manoeuvres of the enemy forces. But guerrilla fighters do not act like a regular army: they do not concentrate their forces in the same fashion, and can move among the civilian population like 'fish in water'. In such conditions, strategic reconnaissance was completely useless and the Italian airmen had to invent new missions for themselves. Hence the initiative of Giulio Gavotti. It would have a long posterity.

Tripoli, 1 November 2011. NATO planes had stopped their bombing a day ago. The air strikes on Libya, which had begun on 19 March, ended on 31 October, one day short of a century since the very first bombing by plane. By a strange historical and geographical coincidence, the bombs launched by the NATO planes fell in the same places as those of Gavotti a hundred years earlier. History repeated itself, seeming to invite us to revisit a century of air bombardments. The historiography of air warfare, which has focused above all on the question of the legitimacy and utility of strategic bombing in the Second World War, finds it hard to take into account the importance of the colonial precedent, most often viewed as simply a 'dress rehearsal' before the 'real war' between the great powers.[1] Yet the history of air bombing is full of this kind of 'geographical coincidence': the regions subjected to such bombing in the inter-war years particularly included Iraq, Syria, and the Indian 'north-west frontier': Afghanistan and the tribal regions of Pakistan.

What, then, happened on 1 November 1911?

> I saw two encampments close to a white building, the first with about two hundred men, the second with some fifty. Just before reaching them I took the bomb in my right hand; I removed the safety pin with my teeth and let the bomb fall from the aircraft. I managed to follow it for a few seconds with my eyes before it disappeared. Soon after, I saw a dark cloud rise from the centre of the smaller camp. I had aimed at the larger one but I was lucky. I was spot on.

When he activated the detonator with his teeth, Gavotti did more than experiment with a new way of launching bombs: he revolutionized warfare. It is only today that we are beginning to measure the scope of the revolution commenced in the Libyan sky. Having left on a reconnaissance mission, Gavotti struck an encampment of fighters. This historical first of dropping a bomb from the air resembled in some respects an artillery action, but with the difference that the forces Gavotti targeted were not officially engaged in battle. Besides, Aïn Zara was not simply a gathering point for potential insurgents: the oasis was also a social and economic system. This was precisely the novelty: by dropping

---

1 The military historian Patrick Facon, for example, in *Le Bombardement stratégique* (Monaco: Le Rocher, 1995), deals with colonial wars, the Spanish civil war, and the Japanese war in China in a short chapter of four and a half pages (90–5), precisely titled 'The dress rehearsal'.

a bomb on Aïn Zara, Gavotti did not just hit a target, he actually constituted a new type of target. A hybrid target, which indifferently mingled civilian and military objectives and, among the latter, regular and irregular forces. In this way Gavotti inaugurated a new way of thinking about and making war, the hybrid and 'asymmetrical' wars that have been an obsession ever since.

It is the spectacularly innovative aspect of this event that strategic thinking has focused on: with aircraft it became possible to strike not only armed forces but an entire socio-economic system. It was in no way surprising, therefore, that air power should have been viewed as a solution to the war of position of 1914–18. The unprecedented development of weaponry in the early years of the century seemed to have ruled out completely any kind of offensive. Faced with the impossibility of breaking the front, aviation made it possible to get round it and strike no longer the military forces deployed but the very sources of their power: industrial production, means of transport, political cohesion, and popular morale. Faced with tactical stalemate on the front, aviation offered the possibility of waging a strategic offensive.

Aerial bombing thus became an essential element of 'total war' in Europe in the first half of the twentieth century. From Guernica to Dresden, by way of Coventry, Rotterdam, and Brest, European memories of the Second World War are marked by the experience of bombed cities. The ravages of this war are still well anchored in European 'communicative memory',[2] and recent historiography has

---

2 In the terminology proposed by Jan Assmann, 'Kollektives und kulturelles Gedächtnis. Zur Phänomenologie und Funktionalität von Gegen-Erinnerung', in Ulrich Borsdorf and Heinrich T. Grüttner (eds), *Orte der Erinnerung. Denkmal, Gedenkstätte, Museum,* Frankfurt: Campus, 1999, 13–32.

conducted important work, particularly on the strategic bombing of Germany and Japan. This chapter in the
history of air warfare had long been avoided, seeming as it
did to mark a dilemma in terms of historiographical ethics:
was it permissible to place at the centre of analysis the
deliberate attack on German civilians during the Second
World War? The history of air warfare was thus caught in
a normative cul-de-sac.

To escape from this means remembering Bourdieu's pos-
tulate that the fundamental theoretical operation in social
sciences lies in the definition of the object.[3] We can note
therefore that the normative question surreptitiously intro-
duces a theoretical decision that is anything but anodyne:
to situate strategic bombing solely in the context of total
war in Europe. Yet bombing from the air did not start in
Europe but in the Libyan desert, before striking the Middle
East, Waziristan, Africa, the Philippines, and Nicaragua.
Before reaching the centre, bombing was experimented
with and perfected on the periphery of the world system;
before European cities were transformed into fields of
ruins, there was the colonial matrix of total war.

Although it was only in the 1920s that the systematic
destruction of socio-economic resources was integrated
into the corpus of military doctrine, it was already virtually
present in the bombing of Aïn Zara. Air war thus corrobo-
rates Hannah Arendt's thesis that colonialism provided the
model for totalitarianism, and particularly for the totalization of war. In other words, air bombing does not relate
just to the memory of European peoples, it forms an essential chapter of what is nowadays called 'global history'.
This approach was born from an idea that is simple in
appearance: that the world is one, and that everything

3 Pierre Bourdieu, *The State Nobility: Elite Schools in the Field of
Power*, Cambridge: Polity, 1998, 131.

that happens in one part of the globe inevitably has effects on the 'world system' as a whole. To adopt a 'global' perspective also implies contextualizing differently the value judgements that underlie any theoretical analysis.[4]

Accordingly, far from beginning with the Second World War, air strikes were already part of the arsenal deployed by all the great powers in the colonies. The Royal Air Force promised to render the same service as ground forces but at lower cost: to tame the anti-colonial revolts that were shaking these territories. The concept of 'police bombing' was born. Designed to restore order, air strikes were no longer a practice of warfare, but rather one of 'policing', even 'imperial policing': they were practised not within the frontiers of a state, but on a global scale, as a means of governing the world. The order thus imposed was not that of a particular political sovereignty, but rather that of an entire world system. This book proposes to follow the evolution of this government of the world, from the early twentieth century through to today, taking as its guiding threat the privileged instrument of this: air bombing with 'police' objectives.

'Police bombing' was employed first of all in Iraq. Initially the method chosen was that of a man-hunt, machine-gunning anti-colonial fighters from the plane. But as insurgents often managed to hide, the airmen, out of frustration, aimed their machine guns at cattle. This gave rise to a brilliant idea: instead of hunting down rebels, cut off their resources; and if they cannot be killed, make them die anyway, from hunger, thirst, or disease. This strategic diagnosis was thus not very different from what would be applied in Europe, where, rather than attacking the enemy directly, the preference was to attack the sources of his

---

4 Michel Foucault, *Security, Territory, Population: Lectures at the Collège de France, 1977–1978*, London: Picador, 2009, 3.

power. In both cases, the approach is indirect. Maritime blockade had already played a major role in the collapse of the Central Powers during the First World War, and the Royal Air Force now invented by analogy the concept of 'air blockade'. Operations began with several days of heavy bombardment. The intensity of the attacks then diminished, but remained sufficiently strong to keep the insurgent tribes away from their villages, fields, pasturage, and water sources. The objective of the bombing was to destroy the social and economic life of rebel populations, in order to 'dry up' the milieu in which the insurgents waged their combat.

The history of warfare in the twentieth century was marked by a radical transformation in the relationship between opposing forces, of which 'police bombing' was the most manifest sign. In the classic conception of war, occupation of territory is in both senses the *end* of military action. The victor occupies the territory of the vanquished, appropriates it, and pacifies it. As executive sovereign, he establishes a relationship of protection and obedience with the civilian population. War by air bombing undoes this connection. Occupation of the ground is no longer an objective, since bombing is precisely designed as a substitute for occupation. By the same token, occupation no longer means an end to war. The air force is the favoured arm of the 'endless' wars we know today, wars that do not speak their name, but are presented simply as police operations on the world scale.

The colonized peoples were the target of the first air attacks, using either bombs, machine guns or poison gas. It was not insurgents that these aimed at but rather whole populations, and through them an entire social and economic structure. In this sense, such practices reflect the dominant approach in 'small wars', which, as opposed to 'real' wars, in which one state opposes another, aims not to defeat an army but to terrorize a population. From this point of view, colonial air attack simply extended existing practices, attacking civilian populations to punish them collectively, or even exterminate them. With the advent of aviation, however, the principles of 'small' wars could be applied to major warfare. This would no longer be a matter of striking enemy armies, but rather peoples, exactly as had been the habit in the colonies.

How should we understand this extension of colonial practices to the world population as a whole? A comparison between air strategies on the colonial periphery and in Europe brings a response that is both obvious and disturbing: in both cases, war is the business of a whole people and no longer simply a matter for the state, as a transcendent entity in relation to its citizens. War is 'democratized': if all citizens take part in the war effort, in one way or another, it is absurd to target only those who wield arms and spare those who make possible the use of these by their everyday work. Death in war is no longer the aristocratic privilege of the warrior; it is 'democratized' and becomes accessible to all.

Furthermore, since the people now have the possibility of influencing the military actions of their governments, whether electorally or by strikes, it would be doubly illogical to spare them. Civilians are as important as soldiers in the war effort, and as citizens, they collectively constitute the sovereign against whom war is waged. In a democracy, the population is at the same time an active part of the war effort and responsible for the actions of the government. The bomb launched from a plane is in a sense the democratic weapon par excellence: it can strike each and every one, *omnes et singulatim*, the people and the citizen. With the qualification that some are more a part of this 'people' than others, given that class differentiation holds a determining place in air strategy. Anyone may be a potential target, but it is workers above all who are singled out, for reasons both technological and political.

Working-class districts, more densely populated than the bourgeois quarters and less well protected against fire, were particularly suited to the incendiary bombs dropped in the Second World War. On top of such technical considerations, air strategy was guided by the idea that the working class, a key segment of the war effort, was also the least integrated part of the population politically. Behind the strategy of the burned-out city, therefore, lay a 'revolutionary' perspective, whose ultimate aim was to trigger a working-class revolt against the existing government. If war had become the business of the 'people', then targeting the workers revealed the constitutive ambivalence of this 'people'. Who were actually being targeted? The collective sovereign, that unified political body that is the *subject* of politics? Or, on the contrary, the 'common people', those fringes of the population who can only be the *object* of politics?

If the object of air war is that paradoxical entity, the democratic 'people' – both unified political body and force of social destabilization, collective sovereign and 'populace' – this involves two complementary strategies towards this object, one offensive and the other defensive. On the offensive side, the enemy people are bombed in order to destroy their unity with a view to releasing the forces of anarchy and revolt. In Europe, the people were essentially conceived by reference to the state, their form of political organization. Bombing the people meant attacking the state or, more precisely, acting so that the people would rise against the state. Banking on the lack of coincidence between people and state, the air offensive aims to undo the unity of the body politic and reduce it to the status of a 'populace'. The conclusion that forces itself on us is that national war in the strict sense never existed, owing to the fact that, ever since its invention with the wars of the French Revolution, war between nations has always hidden a class war. The uncertainty about the nature of the 'people' to bomb corresponds precisely to this concealed war that works on a nation from within.

Strategists were well aware of this duality, which is why their doctrines of air offensive were systematically coupled with a defensive strategy. If the object, on the offensive level, was to undo the unity between people and state, the policy of anti-aircraft defence aimed to transform the 'populace' into a unified body politic, to actively construct the moral and political unity of a people. A whole series of measures were taken in Europe with a view to strengthening the coherence of the nationalized peoples. The air-raid shelter became the place where the unity of people and state was materially elaborated, but the social system of the bunker could not function without a political and social scaffolding, designed to discipline and train the population and thus integrate them into the nationalized political edifice.

Among these measures, that of 'welfare' had pride of place, a social and democratic state taking responsibility for the life and well-being of the people. The symmetry between life and death, social state and air bombing, biopolitics and 'thanatopolitics', found its perfect expression in the *Rosinenbomber*, the 'candy bomber' (literally 'raisin bomber') exhibited at the former Berlin airport of Tempelhof to commemorate the air bridge of 1948–49. West Berlin, reduced to ruins by Anglo-American bombing, was supplied by air for a whole year. The Allied pilots, viewed until 1945 as 'air terrorists', were hailed as saviours three years later. Killing with fire bombs or maintaining life by transporting food and fuel; or, what comes to the same thing, making a statized people or unmaking them by reducing them to the state of a populace.

This unstable dualism between people and state was not found in colonial bombing, which was thus both a clearer and a more 'modern' scenario than the massive destruction of certain European cities. Clearer, because in the colonies there was quite simply no state apparatus that could be targeted. But above all, the strategy was more 'modern', inasmuch as combatting insurgent groups and their social, economic, and ecological environment directly connected with the global configuration, without the mediation of the nation state. As we shall see, as early as 1864, Victor Hugo formulated the hope that air power would bring universal peace; then H. G. Wells, a Fabian socialist and member of the League for Peace during the First World War, championed a 'world state' capable of intervening militarily everywhere in the world in case of manifest disorder.[5] And, perhaps more surprising, the Italian general Giulio Douhet was not just content to recommend attacking civilian populations from the air using bombs and toxic gas, but championed at the same time a key idea of pacifism, that of an 'international tribunal' that would prevent war by submitting its decisions to sanction by air forces.[6]

'Pilot as policeman, bomb as baton' – this is where the colonial practice of police bombing links up with humanist cosmopolitism.[7] While the colonial project is today largely

5 H. G. Wells, *War and the Future: Italy, France and Britain at War*, London: Cassell, 1917, 275–8; and *Experiment in Autobiography: Discoveries and Conclusions of a Very Ordinary Brain (Since 1866)*, London: Gollancz, 1934, vol. 2, 651.

6 Giulio Douhet, 'Incursione in Utopia' (5 March 1915), in Andrea Curami and Giorgio Rochat (eds), *Giulio Douhet. Scritti 1901–1915*, Rome: Stato Maggiore Aeronautica, 1993, 492.

7 Sven Lindqvist, *A History of Bombing*, New York: The New

discredited, the idea of a military air force with cosmopolitical ends continues to prosper, so much so that it is found in Article 45 of the United Nations charter: 'Members shall hold immediately available national air-force contingents for combined international enforcement action.' Air strikes as not only a 'democratic' practice, but also humanist, cosmopolitan, and even pacifist?

In any case, cosmopolitism, as represented at the institutional level by the United Nations, leads us back to our point of departure: Libya. As distinct from the air strikes of 1911, those of 2011 were motivated not by a 'civilizing mission' but by humanitarian reasons, precisely spelled out by a Security Council resolution. They pertain therefore to what the theorist of 'new wars', Mary Kaldor, has called 'cosmopolitical law enforcement', designed to tackle forces of fragmentation, the erosion of state power, 'identity politics', and 'asymmetrical wars'.[8] And it is precisely these elements that connect the Libyan experience of 1911 with that of 2011: all the factors that the 'new wars' theorists present as bound up with globalization were in fact already at work in colonial 'police bombing'.

In this way, the history of aerial bombing converges with the major themes of twentieth-century history: the nationalization of societies and war; democracy and totalitarianism; colonialism and decolonization; Third Worldism and globalization; the social state and its decline in the face of neoliberalism. From this point of view, the history of aerial bombing offers a point of entry, an '*Ansatzpunkt*' such as Erich Auerbach demanded for a philological

---

Press, 2003, section 74. Lindqvist cites R. P. Hearne, who developed this thought at an early date: *Airships in Peace and War*, London: John Lane, 1910.

8 Mary Kaldor, *New and Old Wars: Organized Violence in a Global Era*, Stanford: Stanford University Press, 1999.

approach to world literature, into writing a global history of the twentieth century: 'a particular phenomenon, the best delimited, the most concrete possible', [9] yet one that makes it possible, in the manner of a transverse section, to draw together some of the salient characteristics of this century. In short, bombing functions as the starting point of a global history. Its ambition is not encyclopaedic, and the history presented here does not claim to be in any way exhaustive. Yet it presents a series of examples that seem particularly instructive for our understanding of the developments in the world system over the course of the past century.

Our wars are increasingly hybrid, conflating civilian and military aspects, regular and irregular fighters. They are also becoming increasingly asymmetrical on the levels of technology and 'morale'. Air strikes, which are unilateral by nature, are situated beyond the classic combat that opposes two equal adversaries. And, despite the very complimentary attributes conferred on it (aviation as the weapon of civilization, perpetual peace, cosmopolitism, and the airman as a knight of the skies), nothing is less chivalrous than air war, which substitutes unilateral strike for combat, and transforms the adversary into a nuisance to be eliminated. We can understand, however, why the strategist Edward Luttwak should see it as the privileged instrument of his 'post-heroic' war: it has no victims (in the ranks of the justiciars), it eliminates the problem of mobilization and, at the same stroke, makes it possible to dispense with democratic debate.[10] In a word, this war is

---

9 Erich Auerbach, 'Philology of World Literature', in J. Porter (ed.), *Time, History, and Literature: Selected Essays of Erich Auerbach*, Princeton: Princeton University Press, 2013, 253–64.

10 Edward Luttwak, 'Toward Post-Heroic Warfare', *Foreign Affairs*, 74/3 (May–June 1995), 109–22.

no longer a war but a police operation. The bomb is not the sword of the knight of the sky, but the deadly truncheon of the global cop.

Just as the activities of police and military forces are increasingly less disassociated from one another, so the distinction between the citizen and the enemy to be killed also tends to be effaced. The targeted assassination of the Islamist Anwar al-Aulaqi offers a good example of this. While it was illegal to bug his phone without the authorization of a judge, this US citizen could be killed by a drone on 30 September 2011 without any legal process or the least judicial control, simply on the order of the president of the United States. The evolution of air warfare thus reveals to the world the convergence between the 'advances' of international law and the pure violence of the state.

CHAPTER I

Land, Sea, and Air

On 25 July 1909, H. G. Wells was doing gymnastics in his garden when his telephone started ringing persistently. With some annoyance, he finally decided to interrupt his exercises and picked up the handset. The message was hard to understand amid the crackling: 'Blériot has crossed the Channel ... an article ... on what that means!'[1] From his fine house in Sandgate, Kent, Wells enjoyed a superb view over the Channel and could almost see Dover, some fifty kilometres to the east, where Blériot had just landed.[2] As Wells had just enjoyed tremendous success with his science fiction novel *War in the Air*, the *Daily Mail* editors naturally thought of him to comment on the historic event: Louis Blériot crosses the Channel by aeroplane.

Wells began to reflect. First of all, he greeted the sporting triumph as a gentleman: 'Mr Blériot has done a good performance, and his rival Mr Latham really did not stand a chance. That is the most important thing for us.' Wells recognized that he had underestimated the stability of aircraft, along with almost all other experts on aeronautics. But as he pursued his train of thought, certain worries arose. The consequences of these flights suddenly struck him as tremendous, fearful, and terrible:

---

1   H. G. Wells, 'The Coming of Blériot', in *The Works of H. G. Wells*, The Atlantic Edition, London: Fisher, 1926, vol. 20, 416–23.

2   David C. Smith, *H. G. Wells. Desperately Mortal: A Biography*, New Haven: Yale University Press, 1986, 136–7.

This event – that this thing invented by a foreigner, built by a foreigner, driven by a foreigner, could cross the Channel with the ease of a bird flying over a stream – poses the problem in a dramatic fashion. Our manhood is now defective … The foreigner makes a better class of men than we others.

Foreigners were cultivated, curious, inventive, enterprising. The British were well brought up but lacked initiative, happy to play golf while the French, Americans, Germans, and even Brazilians rose up in the air. On top of the wound this inflicted on patriotic narcissism, another worry struck the writer. The Channel crossing had needed a combination of will, courage, and technical competence. Blériot was certainly a hero, but a hero of a new kind: he embodied an emerging new elite, a new ruling class ready to assume power. The 'natural democracy' of the English could not stand up against the technological heroes of the flying machines.[3] These dark thoughts beset Wells to the point of bordering on the paranoid. If a Frenchman had flown in an aircraft, was it rational to conclude that foreigners produced a better class of man than the British? Wells may have exaggerated in seeing this flight as heralding the end of a particular political system, and of democracy in general. But, from his point of view, the British political, social, and cultural system was losing ground vis-à-vis its geostrategic rivals, and an unprecedented military danger suddenly threatened a country that had up till now believed itself invulnerable, protected by its island shores. Planes setting out from Calais would soon be able to drop explosives on London. Great Britain had to change its mode of social organization, its educational institutions, with a view to equipping itself with the means to create its

---

3   Wells, 'The Coming of Blériot'.

own class of men capable of matching this technological heroism.

With today's hindsight, we can discern in Wells's delirium the anticipation of the end of a historical cycle marked by British hegemony on a global scale, a shift that would take half a century to complete. According to such a well-informed observer as Eric Hobsbawm, it was not until the Suez crisis of 1956 that Great Britain recovered from the shock inflicted in 1909 and recognized that after the loss of its colonies it was now only a second-rate power.[4]

In 1909, however, the United Kingdom remained the hegemonic centre of the world. It had long possessed the military means to control and secure the great sea routes. As a centre of commercial exchange on a global scale, the hegemon had to be in a position to defend its merchant shipping throughout the world; it had to possess what the American naval strategist Alfred Thayer Mahan called 'command of the sea'. This required two conditions: first of all, a navy capable not only of confronting any other, but also – often more difficult – of effectively protecting its own merchant shipping against piracy. This made it necessary to possess naval bases located on the main sea routes, and ideally throughout the world, so as to be able to refuel and repair ships. The advantage of Britain's island position was clear. Maritime supremacy enabled the dominant power both to establish its hegemony in the world system and to defend the metropolis. In other words, an island hegemonic power that enjoyed maritime supremacy could defend itself at less cost than a continental hegemonic power, forced both to maintain a strong navy in the interest of overseas expansion and a strong land army to defend its home territory. The British army was more like

4 Eric Hobsbawm, *Interesting Times: A Twentieth-Century Life*, New York: Pantheon, 2003, 86.

an expeditionary force to be deployed in the colonies in normal times and on the European continent in times of major crisis, as during the Napoleonic wars or the First World War. As long as Great Britain dominated the seas, its home territory was protected against any attack. The great battles of European wars took place across the Channel, on the plains of Flanders.

This makes it easier to understand Wells's shock. From 25 July 1909, Great Britain was no longer an island, as it had become vulnerable.[5] A hegemonic centre, however, had to be immune from any attack. If 'all roads led to Rome', and if all world trade passed through the City of London, the whole world order seemed to emanate from this centre. The hegemon functioned as a quasi-transcendent instance of the world system. If it represented a haven of peace, a promise of happiness and freedom, it also constituted, more prosaically, a political–social system that Kees van der Pijl calls 'Lockean',[6] after the author of the *Treatise on Civil Government*. Following the 'Glorious Revolution', Great Britain replaced the Netherlands as hegemonic centre of the world system.[7] An original complex of state and civil society was born, with the precocious development of a capitalist civil society, framed by the 'rule of law'

---

5 In strategic terms, a land is an island to the precise extent that it is possible to draw a decisive advantage from this. From this point of view, Great Britain had not always been an island. For a very long time, the Channel was no more difficult to cross than a wide river. It only became a strategic obstacle at the time that the English crown was able to monopolize the means of exercising violence at sea and establish an effective coastal defence.

6 Kees van der Pijl, *Transnational Classes and International Relations*, London: Routledge, 1998, 65–79.

7 Immanuel Wallerstein, *The Modern World System, vol. 2: Mercantilism and the Consolidation of the European World Economy, 1600–1750*, New York: Academic Press, 1980, 245.

and constitutional monarchy.[8] British liberalism rested on a state that was strong, but limited its sphere of intervention so as to allow a margin of self-regulation for the capitalist economy and society.[9] There thus appeared a genuine bourgeois/civil society, 'from which the state has withdrawn after having imposed itself actively and constructively, shaping the institutions needed to permit the "liberal withdrawal from the sphere of value creation"'.[10]

Around the hegemonic centre was a 'semi-periphery', a zone made up of a series of contender states that generally presented 'Hobbesean' features, in the sense that the state played a directly dominant role, with interventions in society that were far more frequent and direct than in the Lockean model. This meant that the ruling class maintained a closer link with the state, functioning as a genuine 'state class' with all the risks of authoritarianism this involved. Finally, around the Lockean hegemonic centre and the Hobbesean semi-periphery lay the actual periphery, colonial or post-colonial.

The spatial distribution of violence on the world scale was arranged according to this tripartite pattern. If violence could be total on the margins of the system, it took a statized form in the Hobbesean semi-periphery. As for the Lockean centre, this passed for a haven of peace, a country open to refugees, the promised land of liberty. But it could

---

8 According to the political scientist Robert Cox, the world system is made up of different 'state/society complexes' rather than of different states. See Robert W. Cox, 'Social Forces, States and World Orders: Beyond International Relations Theory', in Robert O. Koehane (ed.), *Neoliberalism and its Critics*, New York: Columbia University Press, 1986, 205.

9 James Mayall, *Nationalism and International Society*, Cambridge: Cambridge University Press, 1990, 76.

10 van der Pijl, *Transnational Classes and International Relations*, 68.

only appear as such inasmuch as it externalized violence, unleashing this in wars between different rival states or on the periphery of the world system. At all events, the centre was constitutionally invulnerable, and had to be so. The mere possibility of an attack could thus shatter a whole system of representations of the world order. If, to cite Gilles Deleuze, 'delirium is geographico-political', geopolitics is also a matter of perceptions and affects. The division of the world into centre, semi-periphery, and periphery is not simply the invention of world-system theorists, but is actually rooted in our mental structures, sensations, and deliriums. To attack the centre is thus equivalent to shaking a whole world, in a sense both geopolitical and mental.[11] If Wells was driven mad by the idea that London could be taken as a target, what can we say about the consequences of a real attack on the hegemonic centre, such as the United States experienced on 11 September 2001?

Wells's delirium becomes more understandable still if we consider the implications of this arrangement of the world in terms of foreign policy, defence policy, and the conduct of war in general. British foreign policy was conducted on two levels, in conformity with a tripartite division of the world: a policy of aggressive colonial expansion outside of Europe had been paired since the eighteenth century with a policy of balance of powers, collective security, and indirect intervention on the European continent. Contrary to the continental powers, the United Kingdom did not aim at territorial conquest in Europe, with the exception of certain naval bases that enabled it to control sea routes. The British custom was to base themselves on one or more 'contender states' in order to contain others, and those

---

11   See Rey Chow, 'The Age of the World Target', in Paul Bowman (ed.), *The Rey Chow Reader*, New York: Columbia University Press, 2010, 3–18.

European states that were weakest militarily could count on British aid to finance their war effort. The success of such a strategy is evident: out of the seven wars fought with France between 1689 and 1815, Great Britain only lost one, the war of American independence – which was also the only time that it did not succeed in creating a continental alliance against France.[12] In the same way, the First and Second World Wars, which put a stop to the German claim to world hegemony, were won above all thanks to the alliance with the Russian and then Soviet contender.

The conduct of war in general, moreover, depends on the geopolitical distribution of violence within the world system. Since the seventeenth century, European war has been conducted between states.[13] The state first of all puts an end to the 'state of nature' by establishing on its territory a power capable of containing civil war. Internal armed conflicts steadily came to an end. The corollary of this statization was a limitation of warfare: once this was defined as a relation between states, it ceased to denote a relationship between individuals. It followed from this that the latter had the right to be protected from warlike violence. Rousseau only repeated a common opinion when he wrote that, even in war, states were bound to respect the persons and goods of citizens:

> The purpose of war being to destroy the enemy state, its defenders may rightfully be killed so long as they are carrying arms; but as soon as they lay them down and surrender,

---

12   Benno Teschke, *The Myth of 1648: Class, Geopolitics, and the Making of Modern International Relations*, London: Verso, 2003, 259.

13   Wilhelm Janssen, entry 'Friede', in Otto Brunner, Werner Conze, and Reinhart Koselleck (eds), *Geschichtliche Grundbegriffe: Historisches Lexikon zur politisch-sozialen Sprache in Deutschland*, Stuttgart: Klett-Cotta, 1975, vol. 2, 562.

ceasing to be enemies or agents of the enemy, they become simply men again, and there is no longer any right over their lives.[14]

If Europe perceived itself as being de facto united, first of all in a *Res publica christiana*, then in a common 'civilization' or 'society', outside Europe things were very different. In colonial wars, the civilian population was never seen as having the right to a particular protection. Military theorists explained this in the clearest possible terms. Colonel Callwell, for example, a British colonial officer, summed up in the late nineteenth century the principles of 'small' colonial wars:

> The main points of difference between small wars and regular campaigns ... are that, in the former, the beating of the hostile armies is not necessarily the main object even if they exist, that effect on morale is often far more important than material success, and that the operations are sometimes limited to committing havoc which the laws of regular warfare do not sanction.

Since colonial wars did not oppose two states monopolizing legitimate violence, as embodied in an army, the distinction between 'defenders of the state' and 'ordinary men' was not applicable. Thus, a regular war 'may be terminated by the surrender or capitulation of the hostile sovereign or chief, who answers for his people; but in the suppression of a rebellion the refractory subjects of the ruling power must all be chastised and subdued.'[15] In

---

14   Jean-Jacques Rousseau, *The Social Contract*, Oxford: Oxford University Press, 2008, Book 1, Chapter 4, 52.

15   C. E. Callwell, *Small Wars: Their Principle and Practice*, Lincoln: University of Nebraska Press, 1996, 41. See also Lindqvist,

Europe, the enemy was considered as 'just' (*justus hostis*) inasmuch as it was sovereign states and their regular armies that confronted one another.[16] The attribute of justice distinguishes an enemy from a rebel or a criminal. Outside of Europe, on the other hand, the attribute of justice was not applied, and neither combatants nor civilians had this right to protection.

It was thus in regions outside of Europe that most bombings took place. In 1855, the Americans bombed the town of San Juan in Nicaragua, provoking the indignation of the British, who condemned an action 'without precedent among civilized nations'. But this did not stop their own armed forces from bombing Canton the following year. The Chinese had arrested the crew of a British ship. After intervention by the consul, the authorities agreed to release the prisoners, but refused to make a public apology and give guarantees that such an incident would not happen again. The British then decided to open fire. In London, the Liberal MP Ralph Bernal Osborne justified the action in these terms: 'Talk of applying the pedantic rules of international law to the Chinese!'[17]

In the nineteenth century, however, the first cracks already appeared in this binary arrangement, divided between a European sphere, with limited state wars, and a 'peripheral' sphere that was the theatre of unlimited war. Quite logically these cracks appeared on the border between the European centre and the colonized periphery,

A *History of Bombing*, New York: The New Press, 2003, sections 46–7.

16   Carl Schmitt, *Theory of the Partisan: Intermediate Commentary on the Concept of the Political*, Candor, NY: Telos Press, 2007, 30, and *The Nomos of the Earth in the International Law of Jus Publicum Europaeum*, Candor, NY: Telos Press, 2006, 121.

17   James M. Spaight, *Air Power and the Cities*, London: Longmans, Green and Co., 1930, 51.

in the US during the 'second war of independence' and in Russia during the Crimean War. North America, traditionally external to the space of European international law, was gradually assimilated into the sphere of civilized Christianity.[18] As for Russia, it was always situated on the margins of Europe: without being as 'civilized' as other European nations, it was nonetheless geographically close and of Christian religion.[19] During the war that Great Britain fought with the United States in 1812–15, British naval forces bombarded Baltimore, Washington, and other US cities[20] – with the aim, according to the strategist Alfred Mahan – of giving the American people[21] concrete experience of war so as to force their government to make peace.[22] The people became a factor in war but, according to an old point of view that considered them as a passive element, only capable of explosions of sporadic violence.[23] As we shall see, this mode of thinking would structure a good part of air strategy in the twentieth century.

Another approach to a war of peoples was also sketched out during the 'second war of independence'. The future president of the United States, Theodore Roosevelt, observed in 1882 that the British, who customarily abstained from

---

18   Schmitt, *The Nomos of the Earth*, 100.

19   See Thomas Hippler, 'La "paix perpétuelle" et l'Europe dans le discours des Lumières', *European Review of History – Revue européenne d'histoire*, 9/2 (2002), 167–82.

20   Spaight, *Air Power and the Cities*, 24–6.

21   Alfred T. Mahan, *Sea Power in its Relations to the War of 1812*, London: Sampson Low, Marston & Co., 1905, vol. 2, 331, quoted in Spaight, *Air Power and the Cities*, 24.

22   Hewson Clarke, *The History of the War from the Commencement of the French Revolution to the Present Time*, London: Kinnersley, 1816, 74.

23   See Déborah Cohen's excellent work *La Nature du peuple. Les formes de l'imaginaire social (xviiie-xxie siècles)*, Seyssel: Champ Vallon, 2010.

personally mistreating civilians, had particularly targeted places where the population organized into a militia were putting up resistance to the former colonial power.[24] The association between militia organization and bombardment of cities was certainly not accidental: once the population are armed for national defence, they almost logically become a target in war. According to this more modern view, the people are no longer a passive factor but the seat of sovereignty and capable of self-organization. Where they were previously an object of politics, they become its primordial subject. And it was not accidental that these incidents should have taken place at a time when revolutionary wars in Europe had placed on the agenda a new conception of sovereignty, concerning the relation between state and citizens.

These incidents aroused debate on the legitimacy of such actions, and on the laws of warfare in general. Since the mid-nineteenth century was a time of peace in Europe, it was the American Civil War that provided the occasion for the first modern codification of the laws of war. The famous 'General Orders number 100' issued by Francis Lieber on behalf of President Lincoln, and generally known as the Lieber Code, is rich in instructive ambiguities in this respect. Continuing the line of 'national wars' begun in 1792, Lieber laid down that 'the citizen or native of a hostile country is thus an enemy, as one of the constituents of the hostile state or nation, and as such is subjected to the hardships of the war' (Art. 21). Thus, the classic distinction between soldier and civilian no longer applies, once the civilian is a citizen (which in Rousseau's formulation

---

24 Theodore Roosevelt, *The Naval War of 1812 or the History of the United States Navy During the Last War with Great Britain*, New York: Putnam, 1882, 162; also Spaight, *Air Power and the Cities*, 24.

means a member of the sovereign against whom war is waged) and the citizen is a soldier.[25]

Lieber immediately goes on to add (Art. 22),

Nevertheless, as civilization has advanced during the last centuries, so has likewise steadily advanced, especially in war on land, the distinction between the private individual belonging to a hostile country and the hostile country itself, with its men in arms. The principle has been more and more acknowledged that the unarmed citizen is to be spared in person, property, and honour as much as the exigencies of war will admit.

Articles 21 and 22 are based on very different modes of reasoning, 'logical' in the first case and 'historical' in the second. As part of the sovereign, the citizen may be the target of military actions, yet the 'advance of civilization' has imposed the norm that unarmed citizens should be spared. These two developments are mutually contradictory. On the one hand, the political individual becomes a citizen, a quality that implies, among other things, the duty of taking part in defence of the country in case of war – modern citizenship, particularly in the institutional forms of conscript army or militia, thus tends to merge into the armed force of a state. On the other hand, nascent international law sought to separate citizen from soldier, to make soldiers the only legitimate target and grant a principled immunity to civilian citizens.

Another and still more important aspect is that Lieber's 'General Orders number 100' distinguished between land war and naval war, determining that the 'advance of civilization' applied especially to the former. In other words,

---

25 See Thomas Hippler, *Soldats et citoyens. Naissance du service militaire en France et en Prusse*, Paris: PUF, 2006.

naval war is less civilized than war on land, quite simply because the theatres of naval warfare generally lay outside of Europe. Naval warfare had its codes and practices, largely in phase with those of colonial war. The Crimean War, however, marked a break with this point of view. In terms of strategic doctrine, it confirmed a technological development dating from the 1840s, steam shipping, which challenged the distinction between a European sphere of limited war and a peripheral sphere of unlimited war. The French strategic thought of the 'Jeune École' played a key role in the elaboration of the corresponding doctrine.[26]

In 1844, the French naval strategist François d'Orléans, Prince de Joinville, saw steam shipping as a way of re-establishing the glory of the French navy.[27] He had the idea of reviving the old French naval strategy of a systematic attack on British trade by corsairs.[28] While set battle had always been fatal to the French, in the face of the superior forces of the British navy, war against commerce, a 'vital principle for England', had always been crowned with success.[29] Technological progress now made it possible to refine this strategy: steamships differed from sail in being largely independent of meteorological conditions, and so

---

26   On the 'Jeune École', see Volkmar Bueb, *Die 'Junge Schule' der französischen Marine. Strategie und Politik 1875–1900*, Boppard am Rhein: Harald Boldt Verlag, 1971, and Theodore Ropp, *The Development of a Modern Navy: French Naval Policy 1871–1904*, Annapolis: Naval Institute Press, 1987, particularly chapters 10 (155–80) and 15 (254–80).

27   'Note sur l'état des forces navales de la France', *Revue des Deux-Mondes*, 15 May 1844, reprinted in [Joinville], *Essais sur la marine française, 1839–1852*, Paris: Amyot, 1853, 168–9.

28   See Marc Belissa, *Fraternité universelle et intérêt national (1715–1795): les cosmopolitiques du droit des gens*, Paris: Kimé, 1998, 309–13, and 'La guerre de course et le droit des gens dans les débats parlementaires (1792–1795)', *Neptunia* 209 (1997), 22–33.

29   *Essais sur la marine française*, 199–200.

13

could be used to wage lightning attacks on the ports and coastal cities of the enemy nation.

A real strategic revolution was thus heralded, which took shape in two phases, first of all at the time of the Crimean War, then that of the Paris Commune and the advent of the Third Republic. Traditionally, navies had two objectives: in peacetime they served as a 'maritime police', and thus for protection of trade routes against pirates and corsairs: in time of war, they intervened against rival navies. In both cases, the element of the navy was the sea. This is what changed with the Crimean War of 1853–56, in which Russia was opposed by a coalition formed by Great Britain, France, and the Ottoman Empire, and the navy now intervened also against coastlines.[30] Odessa was bombarded in 1854, and Taganrog the following year.[31] In other words, the Crimean War brought an end to the strategic separation between land and sea.[32] The Third Republic saw the second phase of this break. In 1886, admiral Théophile Aube was appointed minister of the navy, and in his person the Jeune École made its entry into French naval strategy. Its protagonists were fervent republicans, ardent defenders of colonialism, and the minister himself had spent the greater part of his career in the colonies.[33] The Jeune École, strongly

---

30 Richild Grivel, *La Marine dans l'attaque des fortifications et le bombardement des villes du littoral: Sébastopol – Bomarsund – Odessa – Sweaborg – Kinburn*, Paris: Dumaine, 1856, 5 and 48.

31 Spaight, *Air Power and the Cities*, 41.

32 Richild Grivel, *La Guerre des côtes. Attaque et défense des frontières maritimes. Les canons à grande puissance*, Paris: Bureaux de la Revue contemporaine, 1864, 43; and, by the same author, *De la Guerre maritime avant et depuis les nouvelles inventions, attaque et défense des côtes et des ports, guerre du large, étude historique et stratégique*, Paris: Bertrand, 1869.

33 Hyacinthe Théophile Aube, *Notes sur le Centre-Amérique (Costa-Rica, Nicaragua et San-Salvador), Vancouver et la Colombie Anglaise*, Paris: Berger-Levrault, 1877, and *La Martinique, son présent*

influenced by the Paris Commune, drew two conclusions from this experience of social revolution: on the political level, imperialism had to open up new markets for France and thereby raise the living standard of the metropolitan proletariat;[34] on the military level, the Jeune École strategists were persuaded that the revolutionary threat could be actively used as a weapon in war. Revolts happened when there was economic misery that state apparatuses were incapable of repressing. As a consequence, their political and military strategy consisted in eliminating misery in the metropolis as far as possible, thanks to colonial expansion, and attacking the trade and social cohesion of the enemy. In a word, the aim of their military strategy was to avoid revolution in France and trigger this in the enemy country.

The Prince de Joinville had already pinpointed two strategic targets in a naval war against England: British trade, and the 'confidence' of the British people.[35] This programme took a more radical turn under the Jeune École. One of the collaborators of minister Aube, Gabriel Charmes, spelled out that 'it is clear that the bombardment of fortresses will in future be only an accessory operation … It will be undefended coastlines and open cities that are attacked above all.'[36] If the first phase of the nineteenth-century naval revolution had abolished the classic separation between land and sea, the second and political phase was to abolish the distinction between military and civilian objectives. This put an end to the firm precept expressed first by the French

---

et son avenir, Paris: Berger-Levrault, 1882. See also Ropp, *The Development of a Modern Navy*, 157.

34 Hyacinthe Théophile Aube, 'La pénétration dans l'afrique centrale', in *La Revue libérale*, Paris: Challamel, 1883, 3–4.

35 *Essais sur la marine française*, 174.

36 Gabriel Charmes, *Les Torpilleurs autonomes et l'avenir de la Marine*, Paris: Berger-Levrault, 1885, 154–5. Charmes systematized his ideas on naval warfare in *La Réforme de la marine*, Paris: Lévy, 1886.

strategist Antoine-Henri Jomini and then reaffirmed by the American Alfred Thayer Mahan: 'The organized forces of the enemy are always the principal objective.'[37] For the republican strategists of the Jeune École, the armed forces were precisely no longer the principal objective. Since the nation was one, the army being the nation in arms and the citizen being the soldier, it was the whole enemy nation that found itself in the firing line.

These strategists naturally feared that the adversary would employ the same means, and had no illusions as to the possibilities of defence: it was impossible to foresee where the enemy would strike, thus impossible to defend coastlines effectively, unless naval forces were deployed entirely for this purpose, rather than in defence of the colonies and trade routes. Clausewitz's fundamental principle, that defence is more economical than attack, thus underwent a complete reversal.[38] First naval and then air, bombardment was thus more akin to techniques generally described as 'terrorist': whereas classic war involved a dialectic of attack and defence, we could say that a terrorist strategy consists in completely abandoning defence in favour of pure attack. The relationship between the terms is reversed, and attack becomes both easy and economical, while defence against terrorism is expensive and immensely complicated.[39] It was also for this reason that it was often in the interest of the weaker side to opt for a terrorist tactic, as France prepared to do in the eventuality of a naval war against the United Kingdom. From now on, the side that struck first acquired a considerable advantage

---

37 Alfred Thayer Mahan, *From Sail to Steam: Recollections of Naval Life*, New York: Harper & Brothers, 1906, 283.

38 Clausewitz, *On War*, Book 6, Chapter 1, section 1.

39 See in particular Edward N. Luttwak, *Strategy: The Logic of War and Peace*, Cambridge, MA: Bellknap Press, 2002, Chapter 1.

over its adversary. With steamships and the possibilities of coastal bombardment, speed became a still more determining factor in war. In all these characteristics, French naval strategy in the late nineteenth century prefigured the air strategy to come: it was necessary to strike quickly, to strike strongly, and to strike a nation and no longer just an army. The adversary had other means of defence than to deploy the same strategy.

Was this the subject of Wells's meditations in July 1909? It is certain, in any case, that at the start of the twentieth century British public opinion began to perceive that the country's island position was in danger. As early as 1903, Erskine Childers's spy novel *The Riddle of the Sands*, depicting secret preparations for a German landing on the English shore, enjoyed great success. The Royal Navy remained more powerful by far than other naval forces, and as long as the threat came only from the sea, all that was needed was a certain vigilance. But Blériot's flight shattered this certainty. From 25 July 1909, the situation had definitely changed. Maritime supremacy, however useful it remained, no longer had any great value in protecting the metropolis. British exceptionality had had its day. What was to be done?

To confront this new geopolitical configuration, the British Empire decided to take the initiative. Since 1887, representatives of the colonies and 'dominions' had met at regular intervals in 'colonial conferences', renamed 'imperial conferences' in 1907. But from 1911, a common foreign policy under British tutelage was established: the Empire was transformed into a Commonwealth. The same year, the United States signed treaties of arbitration with both Great Britain and France. Great Britain, a centre now on the decline, and the United States, en route to becoming the new hegemon, renounced war as a means of resolving conflicts. The two great 'Lockean' powers thus removed themselves from the 'anarchy' of international relations.[40] We could say that the centre of the world was globalized.

At the same time, this hegemonic centre expanded in Europe, since France, formerly the main contender on the Continent but singularly weakened by the lost war with the new German contender in 1870–71, was now assimilated into the Lockean centre. In 1912, a Franco-British naval agreement, bearing initially on a colonial dispute in Syria but rapidly extended to North Africa, sealed the new alliance between the British hegemon and its ancient rival. A new world configuration thus saw the light. In Europe, Germany acceded to the rank of principal Hobbesian contender, and the lines of the Great War were mapped out. On the world level, the globalization of the hegemonic power paved the way for the most striking development in the twentieth century's history of violence: the collapse of the separation between the European centre and the colonized periphery. The coming conflict would not be simply a European Great War, but the First World War.

---

40 Van der Pijl, *Transnational Classes and International Relations*, 73.

CHAPTER 2

Towards Perpetual Peace

The news brutally interrupted the lethargy of the three holiday-makers. They found it exceptionally hard to make sense of the notice written in Italian and published in a local newspaper, the *Sentinella Bresciana*: an aviation rally very close by, on the other side of the lake. The world's most famous airmen were to come and exhibit their flying machines. Franz's excitement was contagious. The three friends, who were staying on the Austrian side, decided to travel by boat to Desenzano and then take the train to Brescia, on the Italian side of the frontier. Arriving in the afternoon, they spent the night at a shabby hotel. On the morning of 11 September 1909, they finally reached the airfield.

Less than a year after finding work as a jurist with the Bohemian Institute for Workplace Insurance, Franz Kafka was not yet entitled to a paid holiday. He had to convince a doctor friend to supply him with a medical certificate to travel to Riva, on Lake Garda, in the company of his best friend, Max Brod, and his brother Otto. A few weeks before, at the end of July, Max had written a piece on Blériot's flight across the Channel. As for Kafka, he had recently complained of the difficulties he had in writing and his doubt about his vocation as a writer. This led Max Brod to issue a challenge: each of the three would write a report on the Brescia rally, and they would then choose the best.[1]

---

1   Franz Kafka, 'The Aeroplanes at Brescia', in *The Penal Colony: Stories and Short Pieces*, New York: Schocken 1971. On Kafka's

This rally was a world event of great importance. The town's hotels were full up, and curious spectators arrived from Rome, Naples, and even abroad. King Victor Emmanuel III was in attendance, and the high aristocracy gathered around his majesty. A number of eminent representatives of the world of culture were likewise present: Gabriele D'Annunzio – nicknamed simply Il Poeta – and the demigod of music, Giacomo Puccini. They had all come to witness the spectacle given by the best aviators of the day: Louis Blériot, Glenn Curtis, Henri Rougier, and Alfred Leblanc, along with a number of Italians, including Guido Moncher, originally from Trentino and thus a subject of the Habsburg emperor, like Kafka and his Prague friends. Moncher, however, 'wore Italian colours, trusting more in them than in our own'.[2]

Kafka saw the representatives of official culture as rather pathetic figures: D'Annunzio, 'short and weakly, dances attendance before the most important men on the committee', while Puccini showed 'a nose that one might well call a drinker's'. As for the aviators, Rougier was 'a little man with a strange nose' who had difficulty in calming his nerves; Curtiss tried with difficulty to read his American newspaper, while Blériot's wife was visibly concerned for her husband. Human and fragile on the ground, the

---

participation in the Brescia meeting, see Max Brod, *Über Franz Kafka*, Fischer: Frankfurt, 1966, 92–5; Peter Demetz, *The Air-Show in Brescia, 1909*, New York: Farrar, Straus and Giroux, 2002; Peter-André Alt, *Franz Kafka. Der ewige Sohn. Eine Biographie*, Munich: Beck, 2005, 194–7; Ronald Perlwitz, 'Die Aeroplane in Brescia', in Manfred Engel, Bernd Auerochs (eds), *Kafka-Handbuch. Leben – Werk – Wirkung*, Stuttgart-Weimar: Metzler, 2010, 127–9; Adriano Caperdoni, *Il volo e l'immaginario: nascità e fine di un mito*, Florence: Firenze Libri, 1997, 25–32; Robert Wohl, *A Passion for Wings: Aviation and the Western Imagination, 1908–1918*, New Haven: Yale University Press, 1994, 110–15.
2 Kafka, 'The Aeroplanes at Brescia'.

aviators only showed their true qualities once propelled into the air by their machines. 'Sit[ting] at his levers', Rougier resembled 'a great man at his writing desk', calmly in control of the technology. Blériot, stoically confronting a technical problem that threatened his performance, was transformed once in the air: now 'One sees his straight body over the wings, his legs are stretched down like a part of the engine'. Henri Rougier, the altitude champion who had reached the height of 190 metres, seemed, at the end of this literary report, 'so high that you had the impression of his being able to determine his position only in relation to the stars'.

Gabriele D'Annunzio had not come to Brescia simply to shine in society, but also to collect material with a view to his next novel. This prodigious child of Italian literature had become famous in 1889 with his first novel, *Il Piacere*, inaugurating the decadent style in Italy. Five other successful novels followed until 1900. In the mid-1890s D'Annunzio became acquainted with the work of Nietzsche, and began to combine psychologizing introspection with the theme of the superman. From the start of the new century, however, his creative energy began to decline, and the decadent dandy sought literary subjects suited to the coming new age. This was his mission in Brescia. He persuaded Glenn Curtis and Mario Calderara to take him up in their planes in order to taste the sensations of flight. D'Annunzio emerged transformed by this experience. He had found the subject for his new novel, *Forse che sì, forse que no*, published the following year, 1910.[3]

Two plots dovetailed here: the first, anchored in the heritage of D'Annunzio's decadent period, depicts the com-

---

3 See Jared M. Becker, *Nationalism and Culture: Gabriele D'Annunzio and Italy after the Risorgimento*, New York: Peter Lang, 1994.

plicated relationship that the aviator Paolo Tarsis had with two sisters and their brother, while the second adopted a virile and warlike tone, that of the modern superman.[4] Tarsis and his friend Giulio Cambiaso had been comrades in the navy. Dreaming only of battle and heroism, they fled from the 'outward discipline' imposed on the military in time of peace. They travelled the East in search of adventures, and in Cairo met a French ornithologist, who 'revealed to them the static sense of three dimensions towards the sky'. Tarsis and Cambiaso then built a light plane in order to join the 'little aristocracy' of aviators.[5]

The plot, structured around the antagonism between decadent love and virile friendship, contrasts three pairs of themes. The first two – woman/man and earth/sky – are classic, but the third – cars/planes – is more surprising and resolutely modernist. The tone of the novel is set by the first sentence, shaken by 'the heroic wind of speed'. In this first scene, Tarsis, in the company of his lover Isabella, drives a car at high speed, 'imagining himself driving not a steed that grazes the ground but a steed that rises up'.[6] Attached to the ground and to his woman, the automobilist hero only rises up in his imagination. In order to realize his truly human – and thus superhuman – essence, he has to detach himself from the ground, and by the same token, from women. It is only by flying that man is 'no longer a man, but Man, man the master of the universe, lord of created things', as D'Annunzio wrote again in the Paris newspaper *Le Matin*. Aviation heralded nothing less than 'a new civilization, a new life', along with 'a profound metamorphosis

---

4 A fuller summary of this novel is given in Wohl, *A Passion for Wings*, 116–21.

5 Gabriele D'Annunzio, *Forse che sì, forse che non*, Milan: Fratelli Treves, 1910, 71–2, 75, and 79.

6 Ibid., 9.

of civic life, whether in peace or in war, in beauty or in domination'.[7] It represented, therefore, a major stake, not simply in the field of war, and still less in terms of sporting records. It promised to revolutionize the whole of intellectual life, and consequently all social and political life as well – including property rights, frontiers, and border controls. Before long aerial cities would be built:

> The republic of the air will banish the evil-doers, parasites, the unwelcome, the whole bad lot of them, and open itself to men of good will. On the threshold the elect will cast off the chrysalis of weight, they will glide and fly.

For us today, accustomed to associating air travel with security checks at airports, long hours of waiting, endemic delays and too narrow seats, all this lyricism seems decidedly out of place. But in the early twentieth century, D'Annunzio only expressed a widely shared sentiment. As far back as 1859, in *The Legend of the Centuries*, Victor Hugo dreamed of an airship that would free humanity from its ills:

> Man finally takes up his sceptre and casts off his stick.
> And we see him fly with Newton's calculus
> Mounted on Pindar's ode ...
> This vessel, built from numbers and dreams,
> Would amaze Shakespeare and ravish Euler.

---

7 Gabriele D'Annunzio, 'À la gloire de l'aviation et de la France. Hymne parlé de M. Gabriele D'Annunzio, le grand romancier et poète de l'Italie', *Le Matin*, 30 April 1910. D'Annunzio's 'either ... or' (*soit ... soit*) may be an Italianism that should perhaps rather be read as 'both ... and'.

Aircraft, a true marriage of science and poetry, would realize the realm of mankind, a fully human age.

> Suddenly like an eruption of madness and of joy,
> When, after six thousand years on the fatal path,
> Brusquely undone by the invisible hand,
> Gravity, bound to the foot of the human race,
> Breaks away, this chain was every chain!
> Everything in man takes flight, and furies, hatreds,
> Chimeras, force, finally evaporates, ignorance and error,
>   misery and hunger,
> The divine right of kings, the primitive or Jewish gods.

The invention of the celestial ship was not simply a scientific revolution, it was a spiritual event: 'It bears man to man and spirit to spirit', even able to 'shine faith into the eye of Spinoza'.[8]

This was the legacy that the poets of the early twentieth century had to contend with. In another literary register, no longer lyrical but resolutely avant-garde, aviation was also the Futurists' favourite subject. The most modernist aspects of D'Annunzio already draw on a literature that celebrates the fusion of man with machine, aviation here being the most perfect realization of this. In *La nuova arma: la macchina*, for example, Mario Morasso sees the machine as a true 'vital force', an 'immense multiplication of life' that possesses a 'barbarian soul'.[9] By fusing with

---

8 Victor Hugo, *The Legend of the Centuries*, New York: G. W. Dillingham, 1894.

9 Mario Morasso, *La nuova arma (la macchina)*, Turin: Fratelli Bocca, 1905; on Morasso, see Piero Pieri, *La politica dei letterati: Mario Morasso e la crisi del moderniso europeo*, Bologna: Clueb, 1993, and Anna T. Ossani, *Mario Morasso*, Rome: Athens, 1983. The chapter of *La nuova arma* on 'The romance of the machine' ends with a fictitious dialogue between a man and a woman in a car, speaking not

man, it gives birth to 'a creature half human, half metal tool; a composite monster'. The development of aviation thus has 'philosophical implications'.[10] These themes would be taken up and systematized by the Futurist movement, founded in 1909 – the same year that Blériot crossed the Channel – with the publication of the 'Futurist Manifesto' by Filippo Tommaso Marinetti:

1. We want to sing about the love of danger, about the use of energy and recklessness as common, daily practice.

2. Courage, boldness, and rebellion will be essential elements in our poetry…

9. We wish to glorify war – the sole cleanser of the world – militarism, patriotism, the destructive act of the libertarian, beautiful ideas worth dying for, and scorn for women.

10. We wish to destroy museums, libraries, academies of any sort, and fight against moralism, feminism, and every kind of self-serving cowardice.

11. We shall sing of the great multitudes who are roused up by work, by pleasure, or by rebellion; of the many-hued, many-voiced tides of revolution in our modern capitals; of the pulsating, nightly ardor of arsenals and shipyards, ablaze with their violent electric moons; of railway stations, voraciously devouring smoke-belching serpents; of workshops hanging from the clouds by their twisted threads of smoke; of bridges which, like giant gymnasts, bestride the rivers, flashing in the sunlight like gleaming knives; of intrepid steamships that sniff out the horizon; of broad-breasted locomotives, champing on their wheels like enormous steel horses, bridled with pipes; and of the

---

of their tormented love relationship (as at the start of D'Annunzio's novel) but of the workings of the internal combustion engine.

10   Morasso, *La nuova arma*, 252, 296–7, 286 and 157–8. 10. *Le Figaro*, 20 February 1909.

lissome flight of the airplane, whose propeller flutters like a flag in the wind, seeming to applaud, like a crowd excited.[11]

It was no accident that this manifesto should end up with a celebration of the aeroplane: aviation constituted a perfect synthesis of all Futurist themes, the contempt for history and attachment to the past, a warlike view of the world, the celebration of technology and speed, ending up with a post-humanist vision of the human body and the machine:

> It is necessarily therefore to prepare the imminent and ineluctable identification between man and engine, which will make possible and perfect an incessant exchange of intuition, rhythm, instinct and metallic discipline … We aspire to create a non-human type in whom moral weakness, goodness, emotion and love will be abolished … The non-human and mechanical type, built for an omnipresent speed, will be by nature cruel, omniscient and combative.[12]

Futurism, the first resolutely avant-garde movement, linked the aesthetic and political fields intimately together[13]

---

11 Filippo Tommaso Marinetti, 'The Foundation and Manifesto of Futurism', in *Critical Writings: New Edition*, New York: Macmillan, 2007, 13–14.

12 Filippo Tommaso Marinetti, 'L'uomo moltiplicato e il Regno della macchina', in Luciano Di Maria (ed.), *Teoria e invenzione futurista*, Milan: Mondadori, 1968, 299.

13 The connections between Futurism and Italian Fascism have often been pointed out. Besides the nationalism, militarism, and anti-parliamentarism common to both movements, a personal affinity between Marinetti and Mussolini led the former to present himself on the Fascist list in the 1919 elections (see Renzo De Felice, *Mussolini il rivoluzionario (1883–1920)*, Turin: Einaudi, 1965, 475). This collaboration came to an end the following year, when the second congress of the Italian Fascist Party cast off its left-wing tendencies. In 1923, the futurist Giuseppe Prezzolini in 'Fascismo e Futurismo', *Il*

with the aim of superseding the human, aviation and the figure of the airman being the prototypes of this. Futurism not only launched into 'aero-poetry' and 'aero-painting', but also into 'aero-cuisine', the promotion of a 'food adapted to a life ever more aerial and rapid', involving above all 'the abolition of pasta, the absurd Italian religion', since 'it is on account of eating this that [Italians] grow sceptical, ironic and sentimental'.[14]

The year after the publication of this manifesto saw the appearance of another memorable text on 'the social influences of aviation'. Achille Loria, professor of economics at the University of Turin and editor of a major intellectual periodical, *Echi e commenti*, was already one of Italy's leading intellectuals, and would be appointed a senator in 1919.[15] Though almost forgotten today, his name gave rise to Gramsci's concept of 'Lorianism', coined to denote a form of stupidity specific to intellectuals, and

---

Secolo, 3 July 1923, stressed the differences with Fascism, which he described as a hierarchical, traditional, and authoritarian movement, whereas Futurism remained fiercely anti-clerical and anti-monarchic (see Walter L. Adamson, 'Modernism and Fascism: The Politics of Culture in Italy, 1903–1922', *American Historical Review*, 95 (1990), 359–90). The political programme sketched in Marinetti's Manifesto of the Italian Futurist Party included a good number of elements that were very problematic for Fascist ideology: a violent anti-clericalism, free love and opposition to marriage, the socialization of land, a heavy tax on large fortunes, limitation of the right of inheritance, the right to strike, freedom of the press, the abolition of the political police and of the state's right to use armed force to protect public order (Filippo Tommaso Marinetti, 'Manifesto of the Futurist Political Party', in *Critical Writings: New Edition*, New York: Farrar, Straus and Giroux, 2008, 271–6). The fullest study of this question is undoubtedly Günter Berghaus, *Futurism and Politics: Between Anarchist Rebellion and Fascist Reaction, 1909–1944*, Providence: Berghahn Books, 1996.

14 Filippo Tommaso Marinetti, *The Futurist Cookbook*, San Francisco: Chronicle Books, 1991, 44.

15 S. B. Clough, 'Loria, Achille', *International Encyclopedia of the Social Sciences*, London: Macmillan, 1968, vol. 9, 474–5.

of which his article on aviation was the ideal-type:[16] 'this article is entirely a masterpiece of "oddnesses"' and, 'given the hilarious character of its content, suited to becoming a "counter-manual" for a school of formal logic and scientific good sense'.[17]

Like D'Annunzio, Loria was convinced that aviation would revolutionize social life, marking the definitive triumph of economic liberalism. Its first victim, protectionism, would succumb 'when goods fall on us like meteorites'. In this way, aviation would realize human freedom in the full sense: 'the tie ... that binds the worker to capital will disappear ... when the worker, reluctant to enter the factory or banished from it, finds an aeroplane or dirigible that will lift him into the air'. But individual morality would also benefit. The rate of criminality in cities and plains is higher than in mountain villages, which proves the moral benefits of altitude. Loria thus recommends the construction of aerial prisons, and 'we shall then see, under the magic influence of the rarefied atmosphere, the most baleful murderers transformed into gentle and pious meditators'.[18]

Given such high stakes as these, it was certainly no longer possible to 'view aviation as a strange and dangerous game, lacking any practical importance and reserved for acrobats and the mad', to quote D'Annunzio once more. On the contrary, it set humanity at a crossroads. By its capacity to free him from the hold of gravity, aeronautics could realize man's true humanity. Technological progress would make

---

16 See also Umberto Ricci's ironic comments in *La questione sociale risoluta coll'Aviazione*, Verona: Società Tipografica Cooperative, 1910.

17 Antonio Gramsci, *Quaderni del carcere*, Milan: Einaudi, 1975, vol. 3, 2321–2.

18 Achille Loria, 'Le influenze sociali dell'aviazione', *Rassegna Contemporanea* 3 (1 January 1910), 21–2 and 24.

him good and benevolent, free, master of himself and the universe. Freed from the weight of earthly phenomena, he could finally realize his spiritual essence. This spiritual and moral idea typical of liberal thought was directly linked with an economic argument, followed by a political one: as humanity would no longer be separated from itself by artificial political borders, men could finally devote themselves to unimpeded global trade. Social conflicts would die down, peace and harmony be established, first of all within one society, then in the whole of the world.

It was not surprising, given this, that the promises of aviation included perpetual peace. Victor Hugo had already formulated this hope. In 1864, from his exile in Guernsey, he wrote an enthusiastic letter to Nadar to congratulate him for his essays on the subject of air travel: 'Release man. From whom? From his tyrant? Which tyrant? Weight.'[19] Aviation meant

the immediate, absolute, instantaneous, universal suppression of borders, everywhere at once, throughout the world … All border posts are abolished. All separation destroyed … All tyranny with no rationale. It means the disappearance of armies, conflicts, wars, exploitation, subjugation, hatred. It means a colossal peaceful revolution … It means the tremendous release of the human race.[20]

As early as the 1860s, Hugo already reached the conclusion – by an intellectual argument on the philosophical level and a liberal one on the economic and political levels – that aviation was the bearer of universal peace. He was not

19 See Stéphanie de Saint Marc, *Nadar*, Paris: Gallimard, 2010, 219–41.
20 This letter was first published in François Peyrey, *L'Idée aérienne. Les oiseaux artificiels*, Paris: Dunod et Pinat, 1909, 47–50.

alone in investing aviation with this power, nor in falling into this technological lyricism. The French astronomer Camille Flammarion said something very similar: 'When the conquest of the air is achieved, universal fraternity will be established on earth, true peace will descend from the heaven, castes will finally disappear.'[21]

At the start of the twentieth century, the heroic age of aviation, this conclusion would be reached by a quite different argument. Aviation had the miraculous power to make war impossible, not because it freed men, bringing them together and abolishing borders but, paradoxically, on account of its destructive power.[22] The liberal vision of peace was followed by a militarist one. The arrival of flying armies made the art of warfare obsolete: mobilization of men, concentration of troops, marches across the countryside, manoeuvres. At the start of the twentieth century, writers already envisaged the destruction by bombs from the air of industrial centres, capital cities, and military headquarters.

This idea was formulated first of all by Jean de Bloch, a banker and financier of Polish railways, in a book which had tremendous influence, *La Guerre future* (the book that gave Tsar Nicholas II the idea for an international disarmament conference, leading to the Hague Convention). In Bloch's well-documented reasoning, the unprecedented increase in firepower had made every kind of classical manoeuvre impossible, inevitably leading to a stabilization on the front. As a consequence, wars would be long, and decided not by victory on the battlefield but by the

---

21 Camille Flammarion, *Navigation aérienne et voyages en ballon. Conférence faite à l'Association Polytechnique*, Paris: Le suffrage universel, 1868, 56.

22 The same thesis is expressed in Charles Fontaine, *Comment Blériot a traversé la Manche*, Paris: Librairie aéronautique, 1913, particularly 108–9.

economic and political collapse of one or more of the warring parties. Bloch was one of the few analysts to foresee the shape of the First World War. Other writers investigated the consequences of aviation for the future of war. In a programmatic work of 1910, *La Conquête de l'air et la paix universelle*, François Mallet brandished the spectre of the massive destruction of cities. In the face of such a danger, only one outcome was possible: peace, general disarmament, and 'the solemn reconciliation of peoples as the conclusion'.[23]

There was thus, on the one hand, the dream of aviation as bearer of perpetual peace, which, by liberating men and bringing them together, prepared the conditions for true freedom and a fully human realm; while, as the converse of this technological idyll, there were warnings against the destructive power of air war and the conclusion that, given that European nations had by and large the same level of technological development and industrial capacity, war would become steadily less likely as it became more risky. What rational government could take the risk of seeing its cities, its industry, and its infrastructure destroyed by bombing in a single night? War could no longer bring any gain, and governments would necessarily end up understanding this.[24] We thus see the beginnings, in the discourse on air war of the early twentieth century, of the future doctrine of 'deterrence'.[25] But whether it emphasized this or indeed the rapprochement of peoples, the thesis of a peace-

23 François Mallet, *La conquête de l'air et la paix universelle*, Paris: Librairie aéronautique, 1910, xi.

24 The most famous writer to have made this argument was Norman Angell, a British journalist, future Labour MP, and winner of the Nobel Peace Prize for 1933, in his essay *The Great Illusion* (1910).

25 See George H. Quester, *Deterrence Before Hiroshima: The Air-power Background of Modern Strategy*, New Brunswick: Transaction, 1986.

making aviation became a common subject: in France, Paul Painlevé subscribed to it, as did Thomas Edison in the United States.[26] Many examples could be given, but the idea remains the same.

Aviation thus sounded the death-knell of war. Perpetual peace could be seen on the horizon and, where this was not the case, the conditions for its advent must be created. And so, after the liberal peace of rapprochement of peoples and free movement of goods, after the armed peace of mutual deterrence, a third idea of peace came into view: cosmopolitan peace. In 1911, the French airman Clément Ader proposed the formation of an air army against Germany. Revanchist nationalism was already coupled with a republican and universalist note: 'the law of extension of great states at the expense of small ones, which will follow its natural development towards the unification of peoples. Military aviation will crown this great event. Will it be by liberty or by despotism?'[27] Combining liberal peace with peace by deterrence, cosmopolitan peace by aviation sought to draw on federative elements to unify the human race. Taking up the famous expression used by Victor Hugo at the Paris Peace congress of September 1849 that he had chaired,[28] the Italian Alessandro Masi held that

26 Quoted in Alessandro Masi, *L'aviazione civile e militare nel presente e nell'avvenire e i suoi grandi vantaggi per l'umanità*, Loreto: Brancondi, 1917, 13.

27 Clément Ader, *L'Aviation militaire*, Paris: Berger-Levrault, 1911, 61. On Ader, see C. d'Abzac-Épezy, 'Clément Ader, précurseur ou prophète?', *Revue historique des Armées*, 184/3 (1991), 65–77.

28 *Congrès des amis de la paix universelle, réunis à Paris en 1849*, Paris: Guillaumin, 1850; also W. H. van der Linden, *The International Peace Movement, 1815–1874*, Amsterdam: Tilleul Publications, 1987, 328–39; Évelyne Lejeune-Resnick, 'L'Idée d'États-Unis d'Europe au Congrès de la paix de 1849', *Revue d'histoire du xixe siècle* 7 (1991), 65–72; André Cabanis and Danielle Cabanis, *L'Europe de Victor*

Towards Perpetual Peace

aviation was drawing the contours of the 'United States of Europe'.[29]

How could aviation assure world peace and unite the European peoples? Paradoxically, by its power of destruction and its capacity to strike everywhere without being hindered by political or physical borders. The development of aviation thus revived an old idea that had always obsessed pacifist discourse.[30] In the fourteenth century, already, Pierre Dubois, 'advocate of ecclesiastical causes in the bailiwick of Coutance under Philippe the Fair', had called for a peace-making European alliance in a programmatic text, *De recuperatione terre sancte*. In order to establish this peace in Europe, Dubois proposed setting up a council of arbiters, endowed with an executive apparatus that would enable them to deploy against any aggressor a *'remedium manus militaris, tamquam iusticia neccessario complusiva'*.[31]

Henri IV's famous 'grand design' for peace in Europe, which Sully, his main collaborator, speaks of in his *Oeconomies Royales*, was presented in quite similar terms. The main objective of the 'grand design' was to establish an alliance against the hegemony of the house of Habsburg. If it could not be convinced to give up a part of its possessions 'by the prayers and gentle solicitations of all other potentates of the most-Christian association', the

Hugo, Toulouse: Privat, 2002; Thomas Hippler, 'From Nationalist Peace to Democratic War: The Peace Congresses in Paris (1849) and Geneva (1867)', in Thomas Hippler and Milos Vec (eds), *Paradoxes of Peace in Nineteenth-Century Europe*, Oxford: Oxford University Press, 2015, 170–88.

29   Masi, *L'aviazione civile e militare*, 21.

30   The following paragraphs are taken from Thomas Hippler, 'La paix perpétuelle et l'Europe dans le discours des Lumières', *European Review of History – Revue européenne d'histoire*, 9/2 (2002), 167–82.

31   Pierre Dubois, *De recuperatione terre sancte*, ed. Ch.-V. Langlois, Paris: Alphonse Picard, 1891, 96.

union would make war on it and subsequently distribute its territories among the conquerors. Once the aspiration of the house of Austria to universal monarchy was broken, a united Christianity would be in a position to make 'conquests ... in the three other parts of the world, that is, Asia, Africa and America', and above all to 'sustain a continual war against the infidel enemies of the holy name of Jesus Christ'.[32] Later on, such famous pacifists as William Penn[33] and the Abbé de Saint-Pierre would express themselves in very similar terms.[34] Closer to our own time, President Theodore Roosevelt, awarded the Nobel Peace Prize in 1906, reasserted this classic idea in his Nobel Lecture of 5 May 1910, in which he called for the creation of a world 'league of peace'. The great difficulty of ensuring a lasting peace 'arises from the absence of an executive power, a police power capable of applying the decrees' of an international arbitration body.[35] Roosevelt's speech had a great resonance in international public opinion: to establish peace, an international striking force was needed.[36]

---

32 Maximilien de Bethune, Baron de Rosny, Duc de Sully, *Mémoires des sages et royales oeconomies d'estat, domestiques, politiques et militaires de Henry le Grand*... in Michaud and Poujoulat (eds), *Nouvelle collection des mémoires pour servir à l'histoire de France depuis le xiiie siècle jusqu'à la fin du xviiie*, second series, vols 2 and 3, Paris: Chez l'éditeur analytique du Code civil, 1837, 430 and 341.

33 William Penn, *An Essay Towards the Present and Future Peace of Europe by the Establishment of an European Diet, Parliament, or Estates*, in *Penn's Fruits of Solitude and Other Writing*, London: Dent-Dutton, 1916, 8.

34 Charles Irénée Castel, abbé de Saint-Pierre, *Projet pour rendre la Paix perpétuelle en Europe*, reprinted Paris: Garnier, 1981, 216; Abbé de Saint-Pierre, *An Abridged Version of the Project for Perpetual Peace*, Sta Venera, Malta: Midsea Books, 2009.

35 *Nobel Lectures, Peace 1901–1925*, ed. Frederick W. Haberman, Amsterdam: Elsevier Publishing Company, 1972, 105.

36 See Sandi E. Cooper, *Patriotic Pacifism: Waging War on War in*

We can see, then, how aviation gave new life to the old idea of a federative cosmopolitanism endowed with an executive power. Rudyard Kipling, a personal friend of Roosevelt and author of 'The White Man's Burden', was the first to develop the idea of a world government founded on air power. In two short stories, 'With the Night Mail' (1905) and 'As Easy as A.B.C.' (1912), the latter referring to an international 'Aerial Board of Control', a body originating in the technical necessity of regulating air traffic becomes a world technocratic government.[37] 'As Easy as A.B.C.' tells the story of three airmen required to deal with the problem posed by a group of activists who perform rituals of democratic politics in Chicago in 2065: they assemble, deliver speeches, pass resolutions. Instead of repressing these actions by air power, the 'Aerial Board of Control' decides to let them carry on – simply ridiculing them by broadcasting this democratic spectacle directly in a comic programme on London radio.[38]

This premonitory story shows one of the possible results of liberal-pacifist cosmopolitism. The eradication of war by a post-conflict liberal polity leads directly to a 'post-democratic' regime that, despite having the means to repress opposition and contestation in all their forms, prefers to neutralize them without violence.[39] Nonetheless, if this is how inoffensive forms of contestation are treated on the hegemon's own territory, we shall soon see how, in other

---

Europe, 1815–1914, Oxford: Oxford University Press, 1991, 114–15, and Roger Beaumont, *Right Backed by Might: The International Air Force Concept*, London: Praeger, 2001, 8–10.

37 Michael Paris, *Winged Warfare: The Literature and Theory of Aerial Warfare in Britain, 1859–1917*, Manchester: Manchester University Press, 1992, 39.

38 Charles Carrington, *Rudyard Kipling: His Life and Work*, London: Macmillan, 1955, 375.

39 Colin Crouch, *Post-Democracy*, Polity: Cambridge, 2004.

parts of the world and other political configurations, far less indulgence is shown.

Aviation thus abolishes borders, establishes political freedom and economic liberalism on the world scale; it makes war impossible and proclaims perpetual peace. At the same time, its enormous destructive power calls for a cosmopolitical framework: the possibility to threaten the lives of millions of people cannot be left to any 'rogue state'. The legitimate use of air power is conditioned by cosmopolitism, i.e., by 'humanity', since absolute destruction presupposes an absolute cause: aviation cannot serve to defend a particular interest, it must be the weapon of universalism, and thus of humanity as a whole. A humanity, therefore, of which those who are bombed do not form part. They are nothing more than a disturbance, an obstacle, a virtual nothing. Hence the necessity to dispatch them in practice, as soon as they rise up, to the nothing that they have always been in moral terms.

CHAPTER 3

The Knights of the Sky

Suddenly the guns fell silent. In the trenches, a thousand faces turned hypnotized towards the sky. Two planes, one French and the other German, were clashing in a ferocious aerial duel. Absorbed by the battle in the air, the fighters on the ground seem to have forgotten their role. The French Chaudron rose above the German Rumpler, opposing each of its manoeuvres, turn to turn, plunge to plunge. The German machine-gunner had even stopped firing: was his weapon jammed? For at least twenty minutes, in rotating spirals, the combatants descended to the ground. Finally the German plane landed on a grassy field. Immediately the gunfire started up as fiercely as before.[1]

René Fonck, who related this scene of one of his victories in his memoir of the war, was the son of an ancient Alsatian family, fiercely anti-German. Having opted for French nationality, they had to leave their homeland annexed after the Franco-Prussian war. René's father died when he was four years old, and as a young man he learned the trade of mechanic before becoming the 'ace of aces' of French aviation in the First World War, with seventy-five confirmed victories.[2] In the following years, the aviator's autobiography became a unique literary genre, and Georges Guynemer, Manfred von Richthofen, Francesco Baracca, and William Bishop would contribute to forging

---

1   René Fonck, *Mes Combats*, Paris: Flammarion, 1920, 64.
2   Corinne Micelli and Bernard Palmieri, *René Fonck. L'as des as, l'homme*, Paris: Economica, 2007.

the perception that we have of air operations in the Great War. This established the imagery of the 'knights of the air', heroic figures who killed only while braving death themselves, and were imbued with deep respect for their adversaries. This war, in short, was a 'duel', a place par excellence for honour and symmetrical battle.

These texts, however, whether autobiographies or hagiographies, were actually governed by a quite different metaphor from that of the duel, in fact that of hunting.[3] The airmen, who very often established a connection between their pre-war practice as horsemen and their aeronautical practice of war, constructed for themselves a character endowed with a sang-froid ready for any test, a predator's instinct, and the patience to await the right moment to attack.[4] The hunting metaphor is clearly distinct from the imagery of knighthood, inasmuch as it implies an enemy both inferior and dehumanized. Fonck, for example, wrote,

> One day we had the good fortune to surprise a reconnaissance plane. It was above the Somme. The river sparkled in the sun, and clouds formed a screen that hid us from the target. Captain Bosc had compared himself a few minutes before to a fisherman waiting to strike. The Boche was unable to fire a single shot, and was killed like many have

---

3 Manfred Freiherr von Richthofen, *The Red Fighter Pilot: The Autobiography of the Red Baron*, St Petersburg, FL: Red & Black, 2007, 40, 153, 155; Max Immelmann, *Meine Kampfflüge, Selbsterlebt und selbsterzählt*, Berlin: Scherl, 1916, 57 and 62; Oswald Boelcke, *Hauptmann Boelckes Feldberichte*, Gotha: Perthes, 1916, 46, 59, 70, and 75; Christian Kehrt, *Moderne Krieger: Die Technikerfahrungen deutscher Militärpiloten 1910–1945*, Paderborn: Schöningen, 2010, 97.

4 Robert Wohl, *A Passion for Wings: Aviation and the Western Imagination, 1908–1918*, New Haven: Yale University Press, 1994, 226.

been since, without having the time to know what was happening. He fell in a tailspin and was lost among the reeds of a marsh.[5]

Far from being honoured as *justus hostis*, a legitimate adversary, the enemy was simply game to be killed. Oswald Boelcke, a German ace in the First World War, spoke of the 'game of cat and mouse', emphasizing the macabre pleasure involved in killing at a distance.[6] In their autobiographies, the figure of the enemy never acquires an individual character, it is determined simply by belonging to the other side, the enemy nation.[7] The airmen of every nation at war describe air warfare as a hunting party, thus a fundamentally asymmetrical relationship, which of course does not exclude the roles of predator and prey being reversed.[8]

How and why, then, did air war come to be represented as a chivalrous duel? At the start of the First World War, the high commands of the warring powers were very reticent at according airmen any particular recognition. Aviation, seen as a sporting practice, aroused above all the suspicion of an army whose pillars were discipline, camaraderie, and esprit de corps. War was not a game, and aerial combat was simply one form of combat among others.[9] But as the Great War was par excellence a confrontation between nations, it was also urgent to offer the population images with whom they could identify, heroic figures who could embody the spirit of the national struggle. This led General Foch, in a communiqué of 4 April 1915, to salute in the aviator

5 Fonck, *Mes combats*, 69.
6 Boelcke, *Hautpmann Boelckes Feldberichte*, 55, 70, 86 and 112; Kehrt, *Moderne Krieger*, 98.
7 See Wohl, *A Passion for Wings*, 227.
8 See Grégoire Chamayou, *Manhunts: A Philosophical History*, Princeton: Princeton University Press, 2012.
9 Kehrt, *Moderne Krieger*, 99–100.

Roland Garros 'a pilot both modest and brilliant, [who] never ceased giving an example of the finest courage'.[10] This led to the forging of the mythical figure of the airman in books and newspapers:[11] 'mythical', as a 'fable', plot, or story could be organized around an individual hero, but also emblematic of the nation to which he belonged, for which he fought and sacrificed himself. This figure contrasted all along the line with the 'tommy' with his steel helmet and hardened muscles, trudging through the mud with very little heroism to escape the industrialized butchery.[12] The airman, for his part, was young, calm, and self-assured, facing with cool irony the mortal dangers to which he was exposed.[13] The myth of the airman thus made it possible to render a new experience intelligible, that of a dehumanized field of battle completely governed by technology, by associating it with an older imagery.[14]

The images of which these aviators' autobiographies are so full, however, stand in flagrant contradiction with the reality of the Great War, in which individual aerial combat was in fact only a very brief episode. When the war broke out, aviation was a new weapon, and no doctrine for its use had yet been laid down. Nonetheless, it played a remarkable role already in 1914. In September of that year,

---

10 Roland Garros, *Mémoires, présentés par Jacques Quellennec*, Paris: Hachette, 1966, 262.

11 Wohl, *A Passion for Wings*, 210.

12 See among others, John Keegan, *The Face of Battle: A Study of Agincourt, Waterloo, and the Somme*, London: Penguin, 1983, and the works of Stéphane Audoin-Rouzeau, *Combattre (1914–1918)*, Amiens: C.R.D.P., 1995, and *14–18. Les combattants des tranchées*, Paris: Armand Colin, 1986.

13 Kehrt, *Moderne Krieger*, 90–106.

14 See René Schilling, *'Kriegshelden': Deutungsmuster heroischer Männlichkeit in Deutschland 1813–1945*, Paderborn, 2002, 255–9, and Pascal Vennesson, *Les Chevaliers de l'air. Aviation et conflits au xxe siècle*, Paris: Presses de Sciences Po, 1997, 59.

the crucial point in the war, French reconnaissance aircraft confirmed that German troops had been diverted from their advance towards Paris to engage in the valley of the Ourcq. Thanks to this information, the French high command was able to launch the manoeuvre that would lead to the Battle of the Marne and thus the arrest of the German advance, then to the stabilization of the front and finally, after four years, the exhaustion of the Central Powers' resources.[15] Once the front was stabilized, the belligerents used reconnaissance planes, tactically in this case, to photograph the terrain and map out the front lines, forts, trenches, and barbed wire, and to fine-tune artillery fire.

Given the importance that aerial observation had acquired, the adversary necessarily sought to prevent this. Reconnaissance planes confronted one another with the aid of rifles, pistols, and still more old-fashioned weapons, before a regular system was developed that enabled a machine gun to be placed at the front of the plane, synchronized with the propeller in such a way that bullets passed through the blades without damaging the machine.[16] This was the birth of aerial combat: from the need to prevent the enemy conducting information missions. Starting in 1915, the warring armies established aeronautical services, within which they formed chasseur units to combat enemy aviation, though these units still lacked a coherent doctrine. According to Manfred von Richthofen, the words of Oswald Boelcke were 'gospel' for the German aviators – which amounts to saying that their tactics remained largely improvised.[17]

15 Williamson Murray, *History of Warfare: War in the Air 1914–1945*, London: Cassel, 1999, 26–7.
16 Lee Kennett, *The First Air War: 1914–1918*, New York: Free Press, 1999, 69, and Murray, *History of Warfare*, 35.
17 Richthofen, *The Red Fighter Pilot*, 97.

This experience led to a number of conclusions that were gradually applied in the course of the conflict. It appeared that air operations had acquired such importance that no large-scale operation on the ground could now be envisaged without freedom of movement in the air. The sky was a contested space, and so tacticians began to emphasize the concepts of air 'supremacy', even 'domination', after the 'command of the seas' so dear to naval strategy. To render the enemy unable to fly in certain zones, even unable to fly at all, thus became a military objective in itself. As a result, individual air combat was gradually abandoned in favour of manoeuvres in large formations, which made it possible to command the sky above the battlefield.[18] The 'knight of the sky' once again became a soldier like any other. Discipline and esprit de corps, the characteristic qualities of the soldier, took the upper hand over the honour and individuality of the 'knight'. Paradoxically, it was for this very reason that a mythical figure was needed. The aviator was a possible embodiment of this need for chivalry.

At the same time, the war on the ground had run into the sand, the front had stabilized, and there would be only insignificant advances and retreats until the armistice. As Jean de Bloch had already foreseen before the war, the tremendous firepower of modern artillery favoured the defensive, and soldiers began to shelter in fortresses and trenches and behind barbed wire. The military doctrines of all the warring powers, however, continued to promote the tactical offensive as the only way to victory on the battlefield: 'to win is to advance', in the words of the Italian tactical manual of 1915.[19] The other high commands

---

18 On the tactics of air battle and its development in the course of the war, see Kennett, *The First Air War*, 63–82.

19 Comando del Corpo di Stato Maggiore, Ufficio del Capo di Stato Maggiore dell'esercito, *Attacco frontale e ammaestramento*

followed more or less the same line.[20] The essential challenge now was to 'motivate' soldiers to emerge regularly from their trenches, simply to get killed by the tens of thousands by machine guns and artillery fire.[21] Heroically braving death now meant consenting to being butchered like a sheep.

The myth of aerial combat emerged at a time when the absence of any tactic of air warfare was combined with military despair: on the one hand, aerial reconnaissance gave rise to combats which were initially duels between two aircraft that encountered one another more or less by chance; on the other hand, all attempts by ground troops to break the front failed in the face of deadly fire. In these conditions, salvation could only be hoped for with a later development, the ability to overfly the no man's land between the trenches and in this way break the paralysis that had seized the battlefield.[22] The infantryman had no better friend than the earth to protect them from a danger that might arrive from anywhere at any time: he pressed against it, it welcomed him, and for a few seconds gave him the sentiment of being protected from mortar shells, a

---

tattico, Circolare no.1919 del 25 febbraio 1915, Rome: La Speranza, 1915, 26.

20 Michael Howard, 'Men against Fire: The Doctrine of the Offensive in 1914', in Peter Paret (ed.), *Makers of Modern Strategy from Machiavelli to the Nuclear Age*, Oxford: Oxford University Press, 1986, 510–26.

21 'Man is only capable of accepting a certain quantity of terror … One of the conditions of success is to endure, that is, to continue wanting to win. The only way to success is to resist nervous erosion' (A. Niessel, *Le Combat d'infanterie: les facteurs moraux du combat*, Paris: Lavauzelle 1909, 45–7). See also S. Murray, *Discipline: Its Reason and Battle-Value*, London: Gale & Polden, 1894, 36 and 41.

22 Aribert Reimann, *Der grosse Krieg der Sprachen. Untersuchungen zur historischen Semantik in Deutschland und England zur Zeit des Ersten Weltkrieges*, Essen: Klartext, 2000, 69.

situation well described by Erich Maria Remarque in *All Quiet on the Western Front*:

> The earth is more important to the soldier than to anybody else. When he presses himself to the earth, long and violently, when he urges himself deep into it with his face and with his limbs, under fire and with the fear of death upon him, then the earth is his only friend, his brother, his mother, he groans out his terror and screams into its silence and safety, the earth absorbs it all and gives him another ten seconds of life, ten seconds to run, then takes hold of him again – sometimes for ever.[23]

Aviation thus crystallized a series of dichotomies: between earth and sky, man and machine, above and below, movement and paralysis, boldness and fear, power and impotence.[24] The experience of trench warfare was more than men were capable of enduring. They began to fantasize the arrival of a saviour to redeem the earthly creature clinging to the soil, revenge him, and raise him to the stars; the aviator fitted this role.

> The airman, for his part, can know, the airman is capable of so many things. He is superior to the enemy, or rather, he is a being of superior order, a further step in the slow evolution of that vertebrate we call man. And while he is there, rooted in the earth – for where to take refuge from the bullets that he only hears whistle? – while his ankles are stuck in the ground, while water fills his boots, while he is there stretched like a marten ready to leap, an idea takes

---

23 Erich Maria Remarque, *All Quiet on the Western Front*, New York: Vintage, 1996, 39. See also Fernando Esposito, *Fascism, Aviation and Mythical Modernity*, Basingstoke: Palgrave Macmillan, 2015, 189.
24 Esposito, *Fascism*.

hold of him: 'No, it is not the sky that is the obstacle, it is the earth, this dunghill on which we are born, on which we are condemned to crawl until we die and fall back into it.'

In another great novel of the First World War, *Outside Verdun*, Arnold Zweig sums up his Lieutenant Eberhard Kroysing's delirium of aerial omnipotence:

And in that moment he reached a firm decision: he'd become an airman. Just wait until this mess was over and everything was cleared up, until an iron fist had knocked the French flat for daring to stick their nose into German territory, and a certain someone would throw in this sapper business and join the air force. Crawling around in the dirt was good enough for the likes of Süssmann and Bertin, men with no fighting instinct, no fire in their punches, old men, He, however, would metamorphose into a stone dragon with claws, a tail and fiery breath, which smoked little critters out of their hideaways – all the Niggls and other such creatures. He'd have a fragile box beneath him, two broad wings and a whirling propeller, and hey ho, up above the clouds he'd soar like a Sunday lark – admittedly not to sing songs but to drop bombs on the people crawling around below, to splatter them with gas and bullets as part of a duel from which only one person returns.[25]

Better than any other sources, literature makes visible the dichotomies that structured not only perception but also, to a large degree, strategic and doctrinal thinking. It also shows us another use of aviation of which the hagiographic sources only rarely speak, being in flagrant contradiction

25 Arnold Zweig, *Outside Verdun*, Glasgow: Freight Books, 2014, 192.

with the chivalrous image of the duel: bombing.[26] There are exceptions, however, such as the 'Red Baron', Manfred von Richthofen, who describes the pleasure he felt in dropping bombs and machine-gunning humans on the ground.[27] It is clear that Richthofen, at least, saw himself not as a knight but rather as a soldier practising his trade of killing without reservation.[28]

Given the rather unsuccessful results of the first bombs dropped before 1914, one may naturally wonder why the idea of aerial bombing was not dismissed right from the start. The answer is a double one, relating to two types of bombing, 'tactical' and 'strategic'. Tactical bombing was first practised empirically, with bombs dropped more or less randomly. It soon appeared that planes could be used as an extension of artillery, to strike targets situated far behind the front, inaccessible to the largest of guns. Since military success on the front depended largely on rail communication and the ability to rapidly bring up men and materiel, the idea of attacking the logistic infrastructure behind the front – storage facilities, railway stations, encampments – was a logical conclusion. Nonetheless, the difficulties in striking precisely were underestimated. To take just one example, between 1 March and 20 June 1915, the Allies tried 141 times to bomb German railway stations, but only hit their target three times.[29] Other attempts were abandoned on account of anti-aircraft fire, were blocked by enemy fighter planes; or failed due to technical problems,

---

26   On the lack of sources for the experience of bombing, see Kehrt, *Moderne Krieger*, 192.

27   Richthofen, *The Red Fighter Pilot*, 92–4.

28   On Richthofen, see Joachim Castan, *Der Rote Baron. Die ganze Geschichte des Manfred von Richthofen*, Stuttgart: Klett-Cotta, 2007.

29   Basil Collier, *A History of Air Power*, London: Weidenfeld & Nicolson, 1974, 53.

or indeed, more commonly, because the airmen simply missed their target. The bombs then landed in the countryside, leaving craters in the Flanders mud.

This tactical use of aviation, known as 'interdiction', was supplemented, particularly from 1917 on, by another use that was also tactical: 'close support', in other words simultaneous attacks by ground troops and aircraft.[30] These operations were both hard to coordinate and dangerous, since the planes had to fly at low altitudes, and the targets, i.e., enemy troops, were in a position to respond. It was the German army that counted particularly on this tactic, which would become the basis of the blitzkrieg strategy after the First World War;[31] the British air force, however, generally rejected subordination to the needs of land troops.

Alongside tactical bombing – whether interdiction or close support – there was strategic bombing, with a completely different history. The term 'tactics' referred traditionally to the art of winning a battle, while 'strategy' was the art of winning a war. Tactical bombing could thus mean the use of bombers in operations that also involved land or sea forces. Strategic bombing, on the other hand, was the doctrine that the air force would be sufficient in itself to vanquish the enemy. The tactical use of bombing was by and large invented, or improvised, during the First World War, before being largely forgotten in the inter-war years, even if its military effectiveness could not reasonably be doubted.[32] Strategic bombing contrasted with tactical bombing all along the line: if it had long been anticipated,

30 For an overview of this tactic, see Richard P. Hallion, *Strike from the Sky: The History of Battlefield Air Attack, 1911–1945*, Washington: Smithsonian Institution Press, 1989, especially 19–20.

31 James S. Corum, *The Roots of Blitzkrieg: Hans von Seeckt and German Military Reform*, Lawrence: University Press of Kansas, 1992.

32 Murray, *History of Warfare*, 96–7.

fantasized, feared, or hoped for, its military utility was objectively more than limited. Yet, despite this ineffectiveness, it was promised a radiant future. How can this paradox be explained?

First of all, in the early twentieth century, it was not absurd to consider that technology would undergo a major development that would supersede all past experience. This technological optimism was inseparably bound up with the imaginary power attached to aviation as the only weapon capable of breaking the battlefield paralysis. Then, the tactical situation at the front, particularly in the West, led soldiers to experiment with all kinds of new solutions. There was thus an element of military contingency. But an improvised solution could only be lastingly applied if it met the global political situation of the European nations at war: behind military contingency, then, there were in the end profound political causes.

As far as the military conjuncture was concerned, the stabilization of the front and the impossibility of breaking it led the belligerents to seek desperately for solutions to escape this paralysis. The first hope was to find such solutions on the front, by using ever heavier guns, tactical bombing, combat gas. It was the Central Powers, geostrategically under siege, who had the most to fear from the stalemate on the front, whereas the Entente, enjoying numerical superiority and command of the seas, could legitimately hope to sustain the war effort longer. It was not surprising, then, that it was the 'contender' that sought to win rapidly and by any means: from the invasion of Belgium, the German forces resorted to ever more violent means and were the first to use toxic gas against enemy forces. But after meeting with repeated failure to break the front in this way, Germany began to envisage other paths, to bypass the front and strike no longer the active armed forces but rather the sources of their power – industrial production, means of transport, and the political and moral cohesion of their peoples.

Aerial bombing falls into the heritage of naval bombing, practised in the Crimean War and in the colonies, then theorized by the 'Jeune École' as a way of checking British hegemony.[33] After France's alliance with the hegemonic powers before the First World War, the role of chief contender fell to Germany: it was thus logical that Germany should be the first to resort to the 'terrorist' methods that French republican strategists had already mapped out. Given the crushing British naval superiority in the North Sea, the German navy only left its home ports for lightning raids on British coastal towns at the end of 1914. One hundred and thirty-seven persons were killed, mostly civilians, and 592 injured.[34] It was from precisely this logic that the military high command developed its plan to attack London from the air.[35]

Until the Great War, the debate between the respective champions of 'lighter than air' (balloons and airships) and 'heavier than air' (aeroplanes) was not yet settled. Some nations, including France, opted for the aeroplane, while others, like Germany, rather favoured the airship.[36]

---

33 The 'Jeune École' also signalled the recently united Italy as a geostrategic adversary to French colonial expansion in the eastern Mediterranean. See Ropp, *The Development of a Modern Navy*, 162.

34 Robert K. Massie, *Castles of Steel: Britain, Germany, and the Winning of the Great War at Sea*, London: Vintage Books, 2003, 319–60.

35 Ian White, 'Airships over England: German Bombing Raids, 1915–1916', *Army Quarterly and Defence Journal*, 126/4 (1996), 410–20.

36 Among other sources, see Émile Reymond, *L'Aéronautique militaire*, Paris: Librairie aéronautique, 1910, 8–10; Jean Orthlieb, *L'aéronautique: hier – demain*, Paris: Masson, 1920, 8–10; John Killen, *The Luftwaffe: A History*, London: Muller, 1967, 12; Winston

Contrary to planes – small, unstable, and with limited range at the start of the war – Zeppelins were able to carry heavy loads of bombs and make the round trip between the front and London. The naval attacks of 1914 shocked international public opinion, and Wilhelm II initially prohibited this type of attack, authorizing it only after the bombing of German cities by French forces at the beginning of 1916.[37] Air attacks were a periodic feature of the rest of the war, particularly in 1917, before it was decided to stop the experiment for lack of tangible military results. Who could seriously believe that the 227 civilians dead and 677 wounded in the raids on London of June and July 1917 could have any effect on the course of the war?[38]

All the same, the enemy nation owed it to itself to respond to such attacks. And this is where military contingency – improvisation and resort to terror provoking reprisals, and so on – is no longer a sufficient explanation, with deep political causes coming into play. Of the two contradictory developments that characterized the relation between nation and war in the twentieth century – the convergence between citizen and armed forces on the one hand, the immunity of civilian populations on the other – the first now gained the upper hand over the second.

Churchill, *The World Crisis 1911–1918*, London: Odhams Press, 1918, vol. 2, 289.

37 Morrow, *The Great War in the Air*, 107–8.

38 See Raymond Fredette, *The Sky on Fire: The First Battle of Britain, 1917–1918*, New York: Harcourt, Brace & Jovanovich, 1966. Ludendorff, commander-in-chief of the German armies, tells in his wartime memoirs that when faced with imminent collapse he also envisaged massive strategic bombing in summer 1918. See Erich Ludendorff, *My War Memories, 1914–1918*, London: Hutchinson, 1919, 700–1; also Klaus A. Meier, 'Total War and German Air Doctrine before the Second World War', in Wilhem Deist (ed.), *The German Military in the Age of Total War*, Leamington Spa: Berg, 1985, 210–19.

It was not just that 'nations' were taken as targets; it was also these that mutually designated each other as targets. It was they that gave rise to strategic ideas and became the primordial actors of political life in the warring countries. To make this clear: strategy was no longer simply the domain of state military apparatuses; the 'nation' – that is, public opinion in the nationalized civil society – now also played its part. To give only a few examples, in August 1915, Alfred Le Châtelier, professor at the Collège de France, called for the bombing of German cities with an armada of at least 1,000 planes, while H. G. Wells held that 2,000 bombers would be needed to demolish the Essen arms factories and destroy the industrial base of the German war effort.[39]

It almost goes without saying that the hopes placed on strategic bombing were totally disconnected from military, technological, and industrial reality, first of all on account of the poor precision of the bombers. The reply of the champions of bombing was that it was enough to dispatch a sufficiently sizeable flotilla to a sufficiently large target – in other words, thousands of bombers to a large city – to be certain of causing damage. None of the nations at war, however, had this number of planes at their disposal. Experience at the front, moreover, showed that planes were far from being as invulnerable as was imagined, and that anti-aircraft defence posed a serious threat. No matter, the prophets of aeronautics exclaimed; if planes did not give the expected result then more would have to be built, 10,000 according to H. G. Wells. Such demands became increasingly far-fetched, especially if we bear in mind that in 1915, only Italy, the weakest of the European great powers, possessed a plane designed specially for bombing.[40]

39 Morrow, *The Great War in the Air*, 97–98, 120, and 132.
40 Murray, *History of Warfare*, 49.

It was hardly surprising, then, that military men initially showed great reservation towards such ideas emanating from civil society. True, a little terror could be useful, and reprisals could be necessary to appease the cry for vengeance; but to base a whole strategy on such inconclusive foundations! The French high command, in particular, for a long time resisted great pressure from politicians and the press in favour of strategic bombing. Their reason was both simple and convincing: since Paris was the only capital of a warring state to lie within the range of enemy aviation, France would be particularly ill-advised to take the war onto this terrain.[41] More profoundly, the whole political and military tradition of the former 'contender' was opposed to this. From Louis XIV through Napoleon to Clemenceau and De Gaulle, France had won European wars by occupying territory.

The tradition of the British hegemon was quite different, maritime rather than continental, banking on indirect intervention rather than on territorial conquest in Europe. When the German air attacks of 1917 provoked outrage in public opinion, the British authorities commissioned the South African general Jan Christian Smuts to draw up a plan of action. The programme sketched out in the 'Smuts report' made the Royal Air Force the world's first institutionally independent air army and gave industrial priority to aircraft production.[42] An ambitious programme was thus put under way to wage a

41 Morrow, *The Great War in the Air*, 98.

42 Neville Jones, *The Origins of Strategic Bombing: A Study of the Development of British Air Strategic Thought and Practice up to 1918*, London: Kimber, 1973, 130–9. See also Frederick Sykes, *From Many Angles: An Autobiography*, London: Harrap, 1942, 215–24, and James M. Spaight, *The Beginnings of Organized Air Power*, London: Longmans, Green and Co, 1927, 126–30.

real strategic air offensive against Germany, a historical first.[43]

In order to homogenize the Entente's air policies and strategies, an 'Inter-Allied Aviation Committee' was established, on which the opposing views championed by the British hegemon and the former French contender confronted one another. Under the combined pressure of its allies and a section of French public opinion, the French side ended up conceding: a great air offensive, envisioned for late 1918, would bring Germany to its knees.[44] But the German capitulation intervened before this campaign of strategic bombing could be initiated. The First World War thus ended with a major politico-military decision, but too soon to try it out in combat. The champions of strategic bombing held that if the strategy of maximum bombing had been put into practice, while it would certainly have caused a large number of civilian deaths, it would also in the final analysis have considerably shortened the war. The zealots of air power thus maintained the counter-intuitive idea that this weapon would have saved millions of lives. What mattered was to do better next time, and immediately bomb the big cities of the enemy state – without being held back by vain scruples.

All the same, apart from the fact that it was not put into effect, this decision left a large number of political questions open, even philosophical ones, as becomes clear in the French opposition to the strategic bombing of Germany in 1918. The resistance of the French, which had been based

---

43 George K. Williams, *Statistics and Strategic Bombardment: Operations and Records of the British Long-Range Bombing Force During World War I and Their Implications for the Development of the Post-War Royal Air Force, 1917–1923*, Oxford University thesis 1987, 56, quoted in Morrow, *The Great War in the Air*, 244.

44 Morrow, *The Great War in the Air*, 344.

until then simply on the vulnerability of their capital, now became more categorical. The country's representatives on the 'Inter-Allied Aviation Committee' made it clear that

> the objectives assigned to this special aviation are not simply military, in the strict sense of the word ... They are of a political order when the morale of the working population is attacked with the aim of reducing production and creating a movement of opinion for peace.[45]

We see the emergence here of a tension characteristic of the 'Hobbesian' legacy of the former 'contender': despite the integration of the citizen into the public power being an integral part of republican ideology, particularly in the form of conscription, the nation ultimately remained in thrall to the apparatus of the state, an entity that despite everything transcended the republican community. To remain with the Hobbesian imagery: if, as the famous frontispiece of Hobbes's book shows, the body of Leviathan is made up of citizens, this is not the case with the hands and the head. The state, in other words, is more than the sum total of citizens, and it is this supplement that guarantees a border essential to the preservation of a non-militarized civil society. To dissolve the military into the political, as the project of strategic bombing recommended, put this separation in peril, and opened the way to anarchy and civil war.

It was for this very reason that General Ferdinand Foch described an institutionally independent air force to be used strategically as an 'irregular organization'.[46] It

---

45 Patrick Facon, 'Le comité interallié de l'aviation ou le problème du bombardement stratégique de l'allemagne en 1918', *Revue Historique des Armées*, 3 (1990), 97.
46 Ibid., 98.

is disconcerting to find that similar reservations were to be found on the part of other Hobbesian 'contenders', in particular Germany and the USSR. The Lockean hegemons, on the other hand, were scarcely worried by political scruples, which may seem all the more strange since, as distinct from their rivals that practised conscription, they had for the longest time refused to integrate the citizen into the apparatuses of state violence. In the 'contenders', the engagement of the citizen in defence of the state, and thus the convergence between citizen and soldier, was an essential part of the model of national integration. And yet it was the hegemons that would bank on strategic bombing, a political technique as much as a military one, which precisely tended to abolish any separation between these two domains and directly target the body of citizens rather than the established force of the state.

CHAPTER 4

The Colonial Matrix

The guards could not believe their eyes. Yet there was no doubt about it: six flying objects in the sky above Mediche. Immediately alerted, Mohammed Abdullah Hassan called together his advisers. What was this? Some faces turned pale, but no one dared speak up, fearing death as the bringer of bad news. One voice finally put forward the hypothesis that these were chariots of Allah, come to take the Mullah to paradise. Discussion began on the probability of such a miracle. It was at that point that a Turk present at the council proposed a different and more materialist inter-pretation. The flying machines could only be an Ottoman invention, carrying messengers from Istanbul to announce that the Great War was over and the Sultan had won. This idea seemed the most likely, all the more so as one of these machines was approaching the *haroun*. Mohammed Abdullah Hassan hastily put on his ceremonial costume and, accompanied by his uncle and adviser Amir, seated himself solemnly under a white palanquin to await the strange messenger. Who was this and what would he have to say? The first bomb killed Amir outright; Mohammed, himself wounded, found himself covered in his uncle's blood.[1] This was on 21 January 1920. The fact that a bomb fell that day from the Somali sky was inseparably bound up with a whole series of worldwide transformations.

Mohammed Abdullah Hassan, son of a Somali sheik, joined an ascetic mendicant order of dervishes before

---

[1] Douglas J. Jardine, *The Mad Mullah of Somaliland*, London: Jenkins, 1923, 266.

undertaking a pilgrimage to Mecca at the age of thirty. It was there that he met the Sudanese Mohammed Salih, who, under the influence of Mahdism, had founded a radical anti-Western Wahhabi order. On return to Somalia, Mohammed Abdullah Hassan, who described himself as a 'holy warrior' (*mujahid*), devoted all his energy to freeing his country from the European grasp and reviving the faith of his compatriots, unhesitating in his use of force against those of them who did not share his religious and nationalist fervour.[2] The man that the colonists called the 'mad Mullah' had, since 1899, been at the head of an Islamic-nationalist insurrection in the Horn of Africa, causing increasing trouble to the British colonial authorities: at least four punishment expeditions were conducted without success in eradicating it.[3]

At the other end of the world, in London, the institutional fate of aviation was under discussion. In April 1918, the British had established the Royal Air Force – known until then as the Royal Flying Corps – as the first independent military air arm in the world. After the armistice, Lloyd George's government, wishing to reduce the military budget, envisaged putting an end to this institutional independence. Winston Churchill, however, at this time secretary of state for air, deployed all his ingenuity to demonstrate the need for a strong air force in peacetime. The British armed forces were traditionally composed of two parts: on the one hand, the Royal Navy, designed to protect the home country, safeguard sea routes, and serve

---

2 Abdi Sheik-abdi, *Divine Madness: Mohammed Abdullah Hassan (1856–1920)*, London: Zed Books, 1993, 47 and 55.

3 R. Gray, 'Bombing the "Mad Mullah", 1920', *Journal of the Royal United Services Institute for Defence Studies* 125/4 (1980), 41–6, and Gerardo Nicolosi, *Imperialisme e resistanza in Corno d'Africa. Mohammed Abdullah Hassan e il derviscismo somalo (1899–1920)*, Soveria Mannelli: Rubettino, 2002.

as carrier for forces sent abroad; and, on the other hand, a land force whose main task in peacetime was to maintain order in the colonies. The best way to justify the maintenance of an air force after the end of the war would be to integrate it into this 'imperial police'. The insurrection in Somalia thus provided a golden opportunity to prove what air power was capable of.[4]

This intervention, however, got off to a bad start. Because of bad meteorological conditions and untrustworthy maps, only one of the six aircraft dispatched to the Horn of Africa managed to locate the residence of Mohammed Abdullah Hassan; four others focused on a secondary target, a dervish fortress; and the sixth plane had to abandon its mission due to a technical problem. Over the following days, the attacks continued day and night, with planes descending to less than 100 metres in order to machine-gun the insurgents. The wounded Mohammed Abdullah Hassan abandoned his quarters and fled far inland, still pursued by the British squadron.[5] Soon afterwards, he died of flu and the Somali insurrection fizzled out.

It was in the colonized periphery that the power of aircraft was demonstrated. Without any other support, they were able to repress any attempt to disturb the global order and restore imperial peace. To phrase this in European military terminology, it was in the colonies that aviation

---

4 Frederick Sykes, 'The Future of Air Power', memoir of 27 June 1918, reproduced in Frederick H. Sykes, *From Many Angles: An Autobiography*, London: Harrap, 1942, 544–54. As early as 1914, in his capacity as First Lord of the Admiralty, Churchill had commissioned a report on the proposal to use aviation in Somalia. David Killingray, '"A Swift Agent of Government": Air Power in British Colonial Africa, 1916–1939', *Journal of African History*, 25 (1984), 429–44, especially 429.

5 Robert L. Hess, 'The "Mad Mullah" and Northern Somalia', *Journal of African History*, 5, (1964), 415–33.

was used as a *strategic* weapon, able to decide the outcome of a conflict, rather than as tactical support for other operations. Why in the colonies? In the early twentieth century, as we saw, the aeronautical imagination renewed the old cosmopolitical dream of the maintenance of peace ensured by an international strike force. Peace, however, is always necessarily based on a vision of just order. What was the just world order for this cosmopolitism? At this time, international justice was conceived as a function of 'civilization' (in the singular), a notion pertaining to a linear historicism in which certain regions of the world are posited as having reached a higher degree of development than others, and by this token have not only the right but also the humanitarian duty to redeem other peoples from their state of inferiority. To sum up, the world was divided into centre and periphery, civilized and barbarians, metropolises and colonies.

The prevailing idea of peace followed from this conception of a civilizing justice. Before expressing the wish for a world police able to guarantee peace, Theodore Roosevelt proclaimed, in his Nobel Prize speech, that 'There are, of course, states so backward that a civilized community ought not to enter into an arbitration treaty with them';[6] and François Mallet spelled out that, since aeroplanes had made war impossible in Europe, they constituted an instrument of universal peace:

As far as the dark races are concerned, however, one may well ask whether these peoples, whose degree of intellectual and moral development is manifestly inferior to that of the white race, were not created to prepare the bed of the

---

6   *Nobel Lectures, Peace 1901–1925*, ed. Frederick W. Haberman, Amsterdam: Elsevier Publishing Company, 1972, 104.

conqueror. Did a merciless nature not decide thus in its works?[7]

Aviation, as we see, harmoniously combines cosmopolitism and racism.

Even before the First World War, the use of aircraft in the colonies became a recurrent theme in treatises on the wars of the future, as well as in science fiction, to the point that it is hard to distinguish the two genres.[8] Fascinated by the possibilities of bombing or machine-gun attack that aviation offered, science fiction authors were naturally inclined to locate such action outside of Europe, and so outside the world in which their readers lived. With this effect of asymmetry assured, Europeans never imagined themselves as victims. Practices of this kind appeared far more justifiable when directed against 'inferior races'. For example, in a book published in 1907, *Berlin-Bagdad: Das deutsche Weltreich im Zeitalter der Luftschiffahrt* ('Berlin-Baghdad: the German world empire in the age of aircraft'), aviation appears as an essential tool for German imperialist dreams;[9]

---

7 François Mallet, *La Conquête de l'air et la paix universelle*, Paris: Librairie aéronautique, 1910, 37–8.

8 See for example M. Hodier, 'La guerre aérienne à travers la science-fiction: Albert Robida', *Revue historique des armées*, 3 (1991), 78–88. The standard work on aviation literature is still Felix Philipp Ingold, *Literatur und Aviatik: Europäische Flugdichtung 1909–1927*, Basel: Birkhäuser, 1978. For the British context, see Paris, *Winged Warfare*, as well as Sven Lindqvist, *A History of Bombing*, New York: The New Press, 2003. For Germany, see Thomas Hippler, 'Krieg aus der Luft: Konzeptuelle Vorüberlegungen zur Entstehungsgeschichte des Bombenkrieges', in Wolfgang Hardtwig (ed.), *Ordnungen in der Krise: Zur politischen Kulturgeschichte 1900–1933*, Munich: Oldenbourg, 2007, 403–22.

9 Rudolf Martin, *Berlin-Bagdad: Das deutsche Weltreich im Zeitalter der Luftschiffahrt, 1910–1931*, Stuttgart: Deutsche Verlags-Anstalt, 2011. See Wohl, *A Passion for Wings*, 76–9, and Ignatius F. Clarke (ed.), *The Great War with Germany, 1890–1914: Fictions and*

and in *Au-dessus du continent noir* ('Above the dark continent'), the Frenchman Émile Driant depicted air missions
designed to punish barbarians who rebelled against the
civilization fortunately brought to Africa by the French
Republic.[10] In England, R. P. Hearne explained in 1910 that:

> [I]n savage lands the moral effect of such an instrument of
> war is impossible to conceive. Such an expedition would
> cost very little, and be appallingly swift in its action; the
> ordinary punitive expedition is an enormously costly affair
> in lives and money, and drags on for months ... The most
> secret valleys, the most secure retreats of the enemy would
> be opened out beneath the ship, and it would be very quick
> work to pour shells into points unreachable by any other
> means. The appearance of the airship would strike terror
> into the tribes ... It will enable an expedition to be made
> with astounding rapidity, it will create the most terrifying
> effect on savage races, and the awful wastage of life occa-
> sioned to white troops by such expeditionary work would
> be avoided, whilst the cost would be considerably reduced.[11]

If the mission of aviation was to bring the world perpetual peace, 'world' in this sense meant only the global power
centres of Europe and North America. In the colonized
periphery it was invested with a quite different mission,
contrary to the first in appearance but complementary
in reality: to bomb and machine-gun in order to repress
any anti-colonial revolt. In what way were the two

Fantasies of the War-To-Come, Liverpool: Liverpool University Press,
1997, 233–47.
   10 Émile Driant, *Au-dessus du continent noir*, Paris: Flammarion,
1911. On Driant, see Wohl, *A Passion for Wings*, 85.
   11 R. P. Hearne, *Airships in Peace and War, Being the Second
Edition of Aerial Warfare with Seven New Chapters*, London: John
Lane, 1910, 183–5. See Lindqvist, *A History of Bombing*, 74.

missions complementary? Precisely because perpetual peace depended on civilization, and the eradication of resistance to civilization was the precondition for pacifying the world. The much-emphasized notion of peace, in fact, should not be confused with the mere absence of war: true and lasting peace, rather than a more or less short-lived truce, was conceivable only within a community of reason, morality, and responsibility, a community itself inseparable from the modern notion of individuality. Since all these characteristics were lacking in the colonized 'children of nature' – hence, precisely, their lack of civilization – it followed that the regime of peace in relation to them was quite different from that which reigned among civilized nations.[12]

The development of aviation was thus inseparable from a racist representation of the world: it brought peace to white people and bombs to the colonized. In actual fact, it is even misguided to make such a distinction between war on the one hand and peace on the other. Certainly, in Europe the two things were opposites, but this was not the case in other parts of the world, where bombing was both the precondition for peace and its corollary. This idea was perhaps best expressed by Rudyard Kipling; 'the white man's burden' means continually waging wars, even savage ones – yet nonetheless, 'wars of peace': 'Take up the White Man's burden / The savage wars of peace.' A 'peace' that was at the same time a crusade for civilization and a war against famine, disease, ignorance, and tyranny.[13]

---

12   See Brett Bowden, *The Empire of Civilization: The Evolution of an Imperial Idea*, Chicago: University of Chicago Press, 2009, and Oliver Eberl, 'Zwischen Zivilisierung und Demokratisierung: Die Exklusion der "anderen" im liberalen Völkerrecht', *Soziale Systeme*, 14/2 (2008), 349–69.

13   'Take up the White Man's burden – / Send forth the best ye breed – / Go bind your sons to exile – / To serve your captives' need ...

To wage this 'savage war of peace' naturally meant combatting those responsible for such plagues: the uncivilized in all their forms, fanatics, tyrants, the incurably ignorant; in other words, those barbarians and savages who rebelled against the civilization brought by the colonial powers. These 'wars of peace' waged for civilization could indeed be extremely savage, all the more so as the classic European distinction between combatants and noncombatants did not apply in the periphery. In Europe the question whether civilian populations should be targeted was discussed during the First World War; in Africa and Asia the question was not even raised. The use of aviation in the colonies fitted into a long history of unlimited violence on the periphery of the world system.

Moreover, the tensions between centre and colonized periphery sharpened significantly after the Great War. This was particularly due to the global character of the conflict and the legacy of global strategy, particularly that of the Central Powers. From the standpoint of the hegemonic powers grouped in the Entente, the Great War should have remained a European war designed to contain the German contender, without affecting the other parts of the world. The Anglo-Japanese alliance of 1902 was clearly a derogation from this general strategic orientation. In 1914, the Japanese supported the Entente's war effort by declaring war on Germany and seizing Tsingtao, the German naval base in China, as the first step in the rapid Japanese expansion on the Asian continent in the first half of the twentieth century.[14] Another strategic bombing campaign – this time

Fill full the mouth of Famine / And bid the sickness cease … Take up the White Man's burden – / No tawdry rule of kings, / But toil of serf and sweeper – / The tale of common things.'

14 Hew Strachan, *The First World War*, vol. 1, 455–65. See also Ian H. Nish, *Alliance in Decline: A Study in Anglo-Japanese Relations, 1908–23*, Oxford: Athlone Press, 1972.

culminating in the use of nuclear weapons – would be needed to halt the progress begun in 1914. For the time being, it was the Central Powers in particular, geostrategically encircled in Europe, that decided to 'globalize' the conflict. The German-Turkish alliance formed a key element in this arrangement.

The Ottomans sought to secure their empire in the face of repeated attacks from the European powers. The French had seized Tunisia in 1881, the British took de facto possession of Egypt the year after, then the Italians annexed Libya in 1911. The shrunken Ottoman Empire, the 'sick man of Europe', remained outside the 'concert of nations'.[15] On account of the geopolitical situation, the Ottomans were opposed to Russia in the Caucasus and the Balkans, and to Britain in the Middle East. Since the enemy of my enemy was considered a friend, a German-Turkish alliance was a natural development.[16] As the Ottoman sultan claimed succession to the caliphate, the Turkish strategy was to bank ideologically on a pan-Islamist alliance against European imperialism.[17] On 23 November 1914, the grand mufti of Constantinople declared holy war in the name of the Muslims of the whole world, with the aim of attacking Russia on its southern flank, taking back Egypt – to control the Suez Canal, the most important trade route in the world – and kindle insurrection in the Maghreb.[18]

---

15 Mustafa Aksakal, *The Ottoman Road to War in 1914: The Ottoman Empire and the First World War*, Cambridge: Cambridge University Press, 2008.

16 See Ulrich Gehrke, *Persien in der deutschen Orientpolitik während des Ersten Weltkrieges*, Stuttgart: Kohlhammer, 1960; Wolfdieter Bihl, *Die Kaukasuspolitik der Mittelmächte*, 2 vols, Vienna: Böhlau, 1975 and 1992, and more generally, Fritz Fischer, *Les Buts de guerre de l'Allemagne impériale, 1914–1918*, Paris: Trévise, 1970.

17 Jacob M. Landau, *The Politics of Pan-Islam: Ideology and Organization*, Oxford: Clarendon Press, 1990, 97.

18 The Ottoman war plan of 22 October 1914 is reproduced

Although the British and French succeeded in defeating this strategy, it remained one of the roots of what would later become 'Third World nationalism',[19] on a par with the right of peoples to self-determination as asserted in Woodrow Wilson's 'fourteen points'.[20] The hopes of decolonization were seriously disappointed by the peace conferences of 1919, the new League of Nations serving as the legitimization of colonialism, with one of its tasks being to divide the spoils between the victors in the form of 'mandates'. In these conditions, it was in no way surprising that a succession of anti-colonial revolts should have broken out during the war and immediately after, which was the setting for the bomb that fell on Mohammed Abdullah Hassan in his white palanquin.

The operation against the dervish movement in Somalia was a great success, and the Royal Air Force could now demand a permanent place within the British armed forces. At the same time, in 1919–20, another insurrection broke out in the North-West Frontier region of India, an insurrection that the British called the 'Third Afghan War' and the Afghans the 'War of Independence'.[21] Here too, aviation helped to counter the insurrection, but it soon became apparent that the mountainous territory was far less favourable to air operations. Several planes were shot down, though this did not prevent the British

---

in Carl Mühlmann, *Deutschland und die Türkei, 1913–1914: Die Berufung der Deutschen Militärmission nach der Turkei, 1913, das deutsch-türkische Bündnis, 1914, und der Eintritt der Türkei in den Weltkrieg*, Berlin: Rothschild, 1929, 101–2.

19 Killingray, '"A Swift Agent of Government"', 430–1.

20 See Erez Manela's excellent book, *The Wilsonian Moment: Self-Determination and the International Origins of Anticolonial Nationalism*, Oxford: Oxford University Press, 2009.

21 See Brian Robson, *Crisis on the Frontier: The Third Afghan War and the Campaign in Waziristan 1919–1920*, Staplehurst: Spellmount, 2004.

from bombing Kabul, then held by the rebels.[22] The air force would be used again in British India, particularly in 1925.

It would also intervene in Africa, for example in Darfur in 1916, against the Nuer in 1920, and during the Egyptian uprising of 1919. Egypt was a strategic point for the British imperial edifice, since a large part of sea traffic between India and Europe passed through the Suez Canal. Backed by Hugh Trenchard, head of the RAF general staff, Air Minister Winston Churchill grasped another opportunity to reinforce the institutional role of the service, as the League of Nations had placed Mesopotamia, recently seized from the Ottoman Empire, under British mandate.[23] The administration of overseas territories was divided between various government bodies, and the Air Ministry succeeded in gaining control of several territories, including Iraq. Churchill and Trenchard promised in exchange to fulfil the same functions as land forces at a lower cost, that is, to ensure 'imperial policing' and put down the revolts that were shaking the colonies.

The British mandate in Iraq considerably strengthened the colonial edifice, in several ways. First of all, the territory served to secure a continental route between Egypt and India, on top of the sea route passing through Suez. There was then another factor, primordial for the geostrategic history of the twentieth century and whose importance has continued to grow. Since 1911, British warships no longer burned coal but oil, making them far more rapid than their

---

22 David Omissi, *Air Power and Colonial Control: The Royal Air Force 1919–1939*, Manchester: Manchester University Press, 1990, 9–13.

23 See Charles Townshend, *When God Made Hell: The British Invasion of Mesopotamia and the Creation of Iraq, 1914–1921*, London: Faber & Faber, 2010.

German competitors.[24] Besides this military advantage, the change in fuel had a political importance. Until that time, a strike by British miners could totally interrupt the energy supply. Their trade unions had the power to paralyse the world's strongest navy, an irreplaceable tool of British imperial domination.

Oil extended the government's room for manoeuvre vis-à-vis the workers' movement.[25] British military capacity thus gained greater independence in relation to class conflict, whereas the German contender, whose ships continued to burn coal and were thus more vulnerable from this point of view, had to make greater efforts to integrate the working class into the national community. The increased independence of Great Britain towards the trade unions, however, came at the price of greater geostrategic dependence on other regions of the world. Since oil came primarily from the Middle East, imperial domination of this region, including its transport routes, became absolutely vital. In short, while the contender made headway on the path of national-social integration of the working class, the hegemon was in a position to impose 'delocalization', replacing English coal by Middle Eastern oil and thus weakening the trade unions.

These developments explain why the Middle East became the pivot of British air control in the inter-war years. According to the plans developed by the RAF general staff, Baghdad would be the hub of an imperial air route connecting England to Singapore via Cairo and Karachi.[26] Ten squadrons, stationed in Baghdad and

---

24 Erik J. Dahl, 'Naval Innovation: From Coal to Oil', *Joint Force Quarterly*, 27 (winter 2000–01), 50–6.

25 Timothy Mitchell, *Carbon Democracy: Political Power in the Age of Oil*, London: Verso, 2011, 59–63.

26 The following paragraph is based on Omissi, *Air Power and Colonial Control*.

supported by just 4,000 British soldiers and 10,000 Indian troops, would be enough to control Mesopotamia, on condition that the bombers were equipped with poison gas.[27] The regime of 'air control' was approved at a conference held in Cairo in March 1921. From 1 October the following year, the RAF took over the colonial administration of Iraq.[28] It kept its promise on the financial side: British military expenditure in Iraq fell remarkably, from £23 million in 1921–22 to £7.1 million the next year, then to £3.9 million in 1926–27.[29] How was the air force able to control an entire territory for such a derisory cost?

Quite simply, because, contrary to the long history of colonialism, it renounced occupation of the ground except for a number of strategic centres. The inspiration for this was found in naval strategy, where a navy can control the sea by holding a few strategic bases. Air control expanded this idea to the land. What mattered was that British companies could extract oil, and that the security of troops and communications was guaranteed. Aside from this, the colonies' inhabitants could do what they wanted. Air control thus constituted an essential step towards the regime of neocolonial domination that we have today.

Administration by air power established a genuine government from the sky, a 'benevolent' government since a distant one, in which the wrath of the masters would fall

---

27 Ibid., 21, and Rod Paschall, 'The Strategic View. Air Control: Iraq, 1920–30', *Quarterly Journal of Military History*, 3/4 (1991), 20–2. It is still not known for certain whether chemical weapons were actually used in Iraq.

28 The territories placed under the authority of the RAF also included Palestine, an interesting case inasmuch as even the Air Ministry had to acknowledge that the project had failed. See Omissi, *Air Power and Colonial Control*, 43–7.

29 Omissi, *Air Power and Colonial Control*, 37.

only on those who openly defied colonial domination. In the first phase, operations were conducted as in Somalia, in a man-hunt with planes and machine guns.[30] The insurgents, however, soon learned how to counter such attacks. They sometimes managed to bring down planes by concentrated fire, but most often they simply hid. This led the airmen rapidly to give up attacking insurgent groups directly, in favour of what the strategist Liddell Hart later called the 'indirect approach'.[31] In concrete terms, this meant targeting farms and cattle, and keeping tribes away from the environment needed for their survival. In the colonies, therefore, as in Europe, the enemy was no longer attacked directly, but in the sources of his power. And since these sources were always social in nature, inasmuch as combatants depended on the population for their livelihood,[32] it was now civilians who were attacked. Aviation thus made it possible to realize the old panoptical fantasy never realized in Europe: '[F]rom the ground every inhabitant of a village is under the impression that the occupant of an aeroplane is actually looking at *him* ... establishing the impression that all their movements are being watched and reported.'[33] A control by panoptical vision and continual threat of annihilation by bombs that Foucault might well have appreciated.

---

30   John Ellis, *From the Barrel of a Gun: A History of Guerrilla, Revolutionary and Counter-Insurgency Warfare, from the Romans to the Present*, London: Greenhill, 1995, 137.

31   See Basil Henry Liddell Hart, *Strategy: The Indirect Approach*, London: Faber & Faber, 1954.

32   See Michael Paris, 'Air Power and Imperial Defence 1880–1919', *Journal of Contemporary History*, 24 (1989), 209–25.

33   A. T. Wilson, 'Note on Use of Air Force in Mesopotamia, based on his impressions during 1918–1920 while acting as Civil Commissioner, February 26, 1921', AIR 5/476, PRO, quoted by Priya Satia, 'The Defence of Inhumanity: Air Control and the British Idea of Arabia', *American Historical Review*, 111 (2006), 16–51, quotation 33.

But aviation also and especially enabled governance by what the British called 'police bombing'.[34] The regulations laid down that planes should initially drop leaflets on insurgent villages, and only proceed to bombing forty-eight hours later.[35] In reality, bombing was often done without prior warning, and since navigation systems were not very reliable, planes frequently missed their target and bombed the wrong villages.[36] Since naval blockade had played a major role in the collapse of the Central Powers in the First World War, the RAF coined a similar concept: 'air blockade'. Villages were bombed in order to cause their entire population to flee. A first phase of heavy attacks was followed by a series of regular attacks of lesser intensity, but sufficient to keep the insurgent tribes away from their villages, fields, pastures, and water sources. The objective of such bombing was to break the social and economic life of rebel populations, to destroy their homes and villages, to kill off their cattle and ruin their agriculture, in order to 'drain' the environment in which the insurgents waged their combat. Insurgent tribes or those accused of supporting rebels then had the choice between submission to colonial domination or death by starvation.

'Police bombing' was in no way a British peculiarity. All the colonial powers resorted to it in the 1920s and thirties. The French, for example, experimented in Syria with

---

34 Roger Beaumont, 'Policing the Empire', *Aerospace Historian*, (January 1979), 84–90.

35 James S. Corum and Wright R. Johnson, *Air Power in Small Wars: Fighting Insurgents and Terrorists*, Lawrence: University Press of Kansas, 2003, 62–6. See also Arthur T. Harris, *Bomber Offensive*, London: Collins, 1947, Chapter 1, section on 'Police Bombing in the East', especially 22–3.

36 Philip A. Towle, *Pilots and Rebels: The Use of Aircraft in Unconventional Warfare, 1918–1988*, London: Brassey's, 1989, 9–55.

a practice similar to that employed in Iraq. Despite strong local resistance, the League of Nations placed Syria and Lebanon under a French mandate. When a Druze revolt broke out in 1925, the French 'Army of the Levant' used bombers for independent missions, just like the British on the other side of the frontier. On the occasion of an uprising in Hamas in October 1925, the French air force struck the city, particularly its urban commercial zones, destroying two bazaars and 114 shops.[37] In the same year, Damascus was bombed. The French also relied on a policy of terror. When he was asked if the civilian population should not be warned before bombing a village, a French officer laconically replied: 'Of course not, you need to terrorize these people.' The British consul in Damascus saw this as 'a sustained policy of frightfulness', designed to terrorize the population and reduce the rebels to 'absolute submission'.[38]

Colonial bombing in the Maghreb, on the other hand, was characterized differently, above all because the adversary was better armed. The Rif republic declared independence in 1922, and its forces, counting some 25,000 soldiers and 100,000 potential partisans, inflicted humiliating defeats on the Spanish in 1921, and on the French in 1925.[39] The French air force less often undertook independent missions, intervening more usually in support of ground troops.[40] This did not prevent the French forces from resort if need be to bombing the civilian population,

---

37 Omissi, *Air Power and Colonial Control*, 193.
38 Ibid., 194.
39 John Ellis, *From the Barrel of a Gun*, 149–151, and Stephen Ryan, *Pétain the Soldier*, New York: A. S. Barnes, 1996, 182.
40 S. Lainé, 'L'aéronautique militaire français au Maroc (1911–1939)', *Revue Historique des Armées*, 4 (1978), 107–120, and Jérôme Millet, 'L'aviation militaire française dans la guerre du Rif', *Revue Historique des Armées*, 166 (1987), 46–58.

described by a British military observer as 'drastic in the extreme',[41] while from 1923 the Spanish obtained mustard gas (yperite) from Germany.[42]

The champions of police bombing were happy to admit that the policy of 'air control' was based on terror.[43] There was nothing surprising in that: these practices perfectly reflected the conception of a 'small war' – a euphemism for colonial war against insurgents, rebels, barbarians – with the aim not to defeat an army, but to terrorize the population. How else can we explain the apparent necessity and normality of terrorizing the civilian populations of the colonies in this way? If there was certainly a share of pure and simple racism here, essentially the view that the life of an indigenous person had less value than that of a European, this is not sufficient explanation.

To cite only one example, the defenders of 'police bombing' included the British general John Bagot Glubb, who could declare in 1960 that in this form, 'British intervention was purely beneficial. It saved a poor, simple and hardy community from the terror of constant massacre, and established a peace which has never since been broken.'[44] At the end of his life, in the 1980s, Glubb continued to say that 'the basis of our control of the desert was not force but persuasion and love'.[45] This Arabophile worked as a British

---

41 'French Morocco. Summary of Events, Summer 1925', *Journal of the Royal United Services Institution*, 479 (1925), 762, quoted by Corum and Johnson, *Airpower in Small Wars*, 76.

42 Rudibert Kunz and Rolf-Dieter Müller, *Giftgas gegen Abd el Krim*, Freiburg: Rombach, 1990.

43 Charles Townshend, 'Civilization and "Frightfulness": Air Control in the Middle East Between the Wars', in C. J. Wrigley (ed.), *Warfare, Diplomacy and Politics: Essays in Honour of A. J. P. Taylor*, London: Hamilton, 1987, 48–51.

44 John B. Glubb, *War in the Desert: An RAF Frontiers Campaign*, London: Hodder & Stoughton, 1960, preface.

45 John B. Glubb, *The Changing Scenes of Life: An Autobiography*,

intelligence officer in Iraq from 1920, his particular task being to indicate targets for air strikes, before he joined the 'Arab Legion' which he commanded during the Israeli–Arab war of 1948, giving him the nickname 'Glubb Pasha'.[46] John Glubb, who revered the Arabs, was absolutely not a racist in the original sense of the term. On the contrary, he subscribed to a romantic view of the 'noble savage' that was prevalent in British imperial intelligence of the time.

This imaginary 'orient' was the complete opposite of the decadence that had taken over Europe. It was a land of adventure where one could still meet proud and generous individuals, bold and cunning, free and faithful to their traditions.[47] For Britain's 'benevolent imperialism', the point was to understand and respect these traditions and these individuals who placed liberty above everything.[48] To understand how the Arab mind worked. An Arab was first and foremost a warrior, in other words the exact opposite of the 'tommy' of the First World War that had just ended. When the well-disciplined soldier emerged from the mud of the trenches, he let himself be led to an anonymous death, meted out on an industrial scale. If an element of heroism could be recognized in this, it was simply on account of his capacity to slavishly endure the dehumanized horror, when the mutilated bodies of the veterans and the minds destroyed by trauma haunted a Europe fascinated by the spectacle of its own decline.

London: Quartet Books, 1983, 105, quoted in Satia, 'The Defence of Inhumanity', 46.

46 See James Lunt, *The Arab Legion 1923–1957*, London: Constable Press, 1999.

47 Priya Satia, *Spies in Arabia: The Great War and the Cultural Foundations of Britain's Covert Empire in the Middle East*, Oxford: Oxford University Press, 2008.

48 The following paragraph draw on Priya Satia's excellent article, 'The Defence of Inhumanity'.

The Arab warrior, on the other hand, was as capable of hatred as he was capable of love; his explosions of anger could follow his most magnanimous gestures. For him, war was still romantic, an 'excitement' whose tragic outcomes he accepted as a fatality inherent to life. In short, the Arabs were different from us, so different that 'they have no objection to being killed', as Hugh Trenchard, head of the RAF general staff, explained to the sensitive souls of the British Parliament.[49] Arabs loved war precisely because it involved a confrontation with death, and as opposed to the effeminate Europeans, they did not make the flabby distinction between combatants and non-combatants. If you thought about it properly, not bombing them would almost amount to insulting their values.[50]

Besides, bombing was particularly appropriate for a population whose 'fatalism' was inherent to their religious and cultural heritage. Fatefully impersonal by its nature, the bomb falling from the sky was like divine anger, requiring not a response but immediate submission. The life of an Arab was thus permanent war, but a war of a quite other nature than that which had just ravaged Europe. Arabian war theory had not yet abandoned the notions of honour and courage. The individual fought freely, proudly, and for his independence. The noble savage was more than a warrior, he was indeed a knight of the desert: 'war in the desert is a constant guerrilla', wrote John Glubb.

Aviation was the weapon most suitable to the Arab art of war, quite simply because air combat presented the same romantic characteristics, because the airman was a knight

---

49   Quoted by Townshend, 'Civilization and "Frightfulness"', 155.
50   John Glubb, *The Story of the Arab Legion*, London: Hodder & Stoughton, 1948, 149, and *Arabian Adventures: Ten Years of Joyful Service*, London: Cassell, 1978, 148, quoted by Satia, 'The Defence of Inhumanity', 37–9.

of the sky as the Arab was a knight of the desert. It was not surprising, therefore, that 'a kind of mutual sympathy existed between these Arab nomads and the air force', as the RAF officer Robert Brooke-Popham remarked. Thomas Edward Lawrence, known as 'Lawrence of Arabia', even saw the 'Bedouin way of warfare' as the antidote to the anonymous massacres of the Great War: 'What the Arabs did yesterday, the Air Forces may do tomorrow. And in the same way – yet more swiftly.'[51]

It was not simply an accident of history that imperial 'police bombing' followed the unsuccessful attempt to wage a strategic bombing offensive against Germany at the end of the First World War. Quite the contrary, the two different types of theatre that were previously radically separate, Europe and the colonized periphery, now inexorably converged. The reason for this is that air forces were equated with the 'guerrilla' that the Arabs had always practised. Aviation, in other words, was the privileged weapon of a war that transcended the state horizon which, for 350 years, had made it possible to limit war in Europe. As we saw in the previous chapter, if General Foch was initially opposed to an air bombing campaign against Germany, it was precisely because he saw an independent air force as an 'irregular organization', a force outside of the state.[52]

'Police bombing' radically transformed the relationship between adversaries. In the classic conception of war, the aim of military action is occupation: the occupying power pacifies a territory by appropriating it in geographical terms, establishing with the civilian population a relationship of protection and obedience. 'Air control' undoes this connection. The practice of 'police bombing' thus signalled a major change in colonial relations, already pointed out

51 Ibid., 29.
52 Facon, 'Le Comité interallié', 98.

by critics at the time: 'Air control can do many things, but it will never be able to civilize or pacify people', Lord Lloyd declared in the House of Lords on 9 April 1930.[53] Colonialism without a civilizing mission? This suggested a serious danger for the legitimation of colonial power.

De Gaulle said much the same thing when he exhorted the military not to forget to keep their feet on the occupied ground: '[A]ircraft can destroy, but cannot compel, cannot conquer, cannot occupy.'[54] This is the paradox of air power, which sows death and destruction everywhere without making possible the occupation, appropriation, and pacification of territory. It thus represents a complete reversal of conceptions of war and peace. According to the classic theory, peace must be the end of all warlike action: war is made so as to obtain peace. How to obtain peace, then, with a weapon intrinsically incapable of pacifying?

---

53   Quoted by Townshend, 'Civilization and "Frightfulness"', 157.
54   Charles de Gaulle, *The Army of the Future* (1934), Westport, CT: Praeger, 1977, 134.

CHAPTER 5

Civilization, Cosmopolitism, and Democracy

He grew up in India, the son of a colonial official, and always dreamed of returning to live in the sunshine. At the age of 16 he ran away from his father, who wanted to enrol him in the military, and headed for Rhodesia. When the First World War broke out, an uncle who was an officer on the general staff managed to place him in the newly formed Royal Flying Corps. Arthur Harris became an airman through nepotism. 'To me it was just an incident pending the suppression of the Boche and the chance to get back home to Africa',[1] he was to write. 'I more or less drifted into the RAF as a regular after the war; I had been in the job so long that I thought I might as well continue.'[2] The job had several advantages for this black sheep whose educational record was mediocre to say the least, including the ability to get posted to the colonies and thus escape the European greyness. But it was once again war that upset his plans, and in 1939 he was forced to return to a Europe that was more dismal than ever and seemed to have finally lost its bearings. The orientalist airmen of the British Empire were convinced that it was in their power to reinvigorate this worn-out old Europe by introducing the cavalier boldness and free individuality that characterized both Arabs and airmen. Arthur Harris would work towards this regeneration. As head of RAF Bomber Command, he was the

---

1 Arthur T. Harris, *Bomber Offensive*, London: Collins, 1947, 16–17.
2 Ibid., 18.

architect of the firestorms that devastated Hamburg and Dresden.

In 1918, however, things seemed to be returning to order in Europe, at least at first sight: the armistice was signed at Compiègne on 11 November. But on closer look, the war was very far from over. The Entente forces maintained their naval blockade of Germany until the signature of the Versailles Treaty in June 1919. The German authorities estimated the total number of civilian victims of the blockade at 763,000, but even if this figure is exaggerated, the effects of the blockade were and remained considerable, in fact being felt all the more after 11 November 1918.[3] Almost everywhere in Eastern Europe, borders were being disputed by paramilitaries, and the fighting there was often extremely violent.[4] Soviet Russia and Poland were at war over their common frontier from 1919 to 1921.[5] The Western powers reacted to the October Revolution with military invention in the Russian civil war, which continued until 1923. Expulsion of entire populations was commonplace, as for example in Alsace and Lorraine, where the French military authorities divided the population into four categories according to 'ethnic' origin and expelled the Germans who held 'D cards'. The violent repression of Communist insurrections often bordered on civil war,

---

3 Charles P. Vincent, *The Politics of Hunger: The Allied Blockade of Germany, 1915–1919*, Athens, OH: Ohio University Press, 1985. Henri Bergson commented as follows on the blockade of Germany: 'Well before England commenced the blockade of its coasts, Germany had blockaded itself morally, isolating itself from every ideal capable of revivifying it' (Henri Bergson, *La Signification de la guerre*, Paris: Bloud et Gay, 1915, 41).

4 Robert Gerwarth and John Horne, *War in Peace: Paramilitary Violence in Europe After the Great War*, Oxford: Oxford University Press, 2012.

5 Norman R. Davies, *White Eagle, Red Star: The Polish-Soviet War, 1919–20*, New York: Pimlico, 2003.

as with the Spartacist rebellion in Germany or the Italian *biennio rosso*.[6] As well as these civil wars and insurrections in Europe, there were anticolonial revolts in Africa and Asia, with the emergence of forms of 'Third World internationalism' as a direct result of the war – often pan-Islamist in inspiration. In 1927, only four years after the end of the Russian civil war, the Communist insurrection in China began. Not only was the war not finished on 11 November 1918, but the 'global civil war' was only beginning: a war on several fronts, opposing political entities and movements of all kinds: liberal democracies, authoritarian republics, Bolshevism, fascism, military monarchies, movements of 'national liberation', supranationalist movements of various allegiance, such as pan-Islamism, pan-Slavism, pan-Africanism, etc.

As far as air strategy was concerned, the First World War ended with a paradox: the Western powers went over to strategic bombing towards the end of the war, although its results fell far short of the hopes placed on it. An inhabitant of Vicenza, in Italy, wrote in his memoirs of the war that the shells of anti-aircraft guns worried the population more than the bombs dropped from planes.[7] And so the question remains as to how, despite all common sense, a strategy came to prevail that was, according to all available indicators, militarily ineffective. The answer is twofold, with both a political aspect and an epistemological one.

The champions of bombing did not deny that, 'objectively', the four years of war had shown the military

---

6 See Giuseppe Maione, *Il biennio rosso. Autonomia et spontaneità operaia nel 1919–1920*, Bologna: Il Mulino, 1975.

7 Giuseppe De Mori, *Vicenza nella Guerra, 1915–1918*, Vicenza: Giacomi Rumor, 1931, quoted by A. Rastelli, 'I bombardamenti sulle città', in P. Ferrari (ed.), *La grande Guerra aerea 1915–1918: Battaglie – industrie – bombardamenti – assi – aeroporti*, Valdagno: Rossato, 1994, 183–250, particularly 189.

uselessness of strategic bombing. Their argument was situated at a different level: they questioned the very foundation of this 'objectivity'. Gathering data to evaluate a policy assumes, in fact, that there is something given and invariable to assess as an 'object'. But this was precisely not the case. For them the meagre results were simply the consequence of insufficient implementation. How could a strategic option be evaluated when it had not been tried to the full? In other words, the empirical data was itself dependent on strategic choices, and if bombing had proved useless, it was simply because it had not been conducted on a large enough scale.

The data collected during the war were also invalid for another reason, as a simple glance at the chronology shows. The first fixed-wing flight, of 37 metres, took place in 1903. Six years later, Louis Blériot was the first man to cross the English Channel, with the type of plane that the French army would use at the start of the World War. This aircraft, with a wooden frame, permitted a maximum take-off weight of 320 kilos and a speed of 73 kilometres per hour. The three-engine aircraft available in 1918, fifteen years after the first flight, weighed 4,600 kilos on take-off, had a range of 600 kilometres, and could reach 160 km/h. What use, then, were forecasts, asked the champions of air bombing, in view of the breakneck advance of technology? The experience of the war had only a very limited value since, on the one hand, the situation was evolving at spectacular speed, while on the other hand, the direction of this development was not fixed in advance but depended on political choices.

The epistemological argument was backed up by a further consideration, more directly political. If there was one lesson to be drawn from the Great War, it was that it had been a 'national' war like no other before it. It was no longer states and their military apparatuses that waged the struggle, but rather entire nations. Conscription was imposed throughout continental Europe, and 60 million Europeans mobilized. The whole of social life was subjected to military needs: industrial production, which was itself completely militarized, now constituted the cornerstone of success on the battlefield.

This new situation had profound political repercussions at all levels. Governments exerted increasingly tight control over social and economic life, even in countries marked by a long tradition of 'Lockean' liberalism. At the same time, the situation also offered leaders of the workers' movement an ideal opportunity to emerge from their pariah status. As we know, however, this opportunity had a price: they had to abandon pacifism and lend their support to the war. In the medium term, internationalism, a key element in every modern politics of emancipation, was deeply affected or even completely distorted. What remained of it would now find its place in the new form of sovereignty of the nationalized social state: transnational class struggle was replaced by a policy of compromise in which social questions could now only exist in a nationalized form. The new 'internationalism' not only adjusted to the form of each particular national-social state, but also to its particular time frame. It was still maintained that the proletarians of all countries would unite. But this would be, if not the work of a miracle, at least that of a 'cunning of reason' that would happen only at the end of an imaginary historical process – itself nothing other than a universalization of the principles in which each national social complex recognized itself. As we shall see, this universalization of principles also formed an integral part of the war mechanism. In other words, the context of emancipation would now strictly coincide with the national contexts of the warring states, and this nationalized working-class emancipation could only be an integral part of the war mechanism. If the First World War was a 'national' war, this was because it was supported by a majority of the population, particularly the decisive segment formed by the working class. And if it was now nations that confronted one another, then the idea of targeting whole nations could appear self-evident. 'From now on, the aim of the war appeared in its full scope and cruel clarity: it had become the destruction not of an army but of a nation.'[8] No matter how paradoxical this might appear, nationalized working-class emancipation formed an essential part of this mechanism.

It was precisely from this point of view that colonial bombing took up the baton of what had already been begun through the projects for a great air offensive against Germany at the end of the First World War. According to a British government memorandum of 1921:

> Great as the development of air power in the war was on the western front, it was mainly concerned with aerial action against enemy aircraft and cooperation with other arms in actions in which land or sea forces were the predominating partner. In more distant theatres, however, such as Palestine, Mesopotamia and East Africa the war proved that air has capabilities of its own.[9]

Arthur Harris may have become an airman out of nepotism, but this geostrategic orientation delighted him: he

---

8   Philippe Pétain, quoted by Camille Rougeron, *L'Aviation de bombardement*, Nancy: Berger-Levrault, 1936, 243.

9   Air Staff, 'On the Power of the Air Force and the Application of That Power to Hold and Police Mesopotamia', March 1920, AIR 1/426/15/260/3, PRO, quoted by Priya Satia, 'The Defence of Inhumanity: Air Control and the British Idea of Arabia', *American Historical Review*, 111 (2006), 26.

could once again escape from Europe. He left first of all for India and the wild borderlands of Waziristan on the North-West Frontier, then for Iraq, where he suffered from the 'dreadful climate' and 'disgusting food', before arriving in Palestine, where he spent 'a year teaching the British army the advantages of air power and teaching the rebels its effectiveness'.[10] But the joy of this colonial aviator would not last. The 1918 armistice had been only a deception, and Arthur Harris was recalled to Europe. Along with him, the technique of bombing, gaily conducted under the blue skies of Africa and Asia, made a sad return to the greyness of Europe; Harris brought with him to the European centre the colonized periphery. How did this come about?

According to the British strategist Basil Liddell Hart, one of the lessons to be drawn from the Great War was that war was no longer limited to a combat of 'paid gladiators', but involved whole nations, whole countries, whole populations.[11] Giulio Douhet, the Italian general who would become the most important theorist of strategic bombing, added that 'the distinction between belligerents and non-belligerents no longer exists now, since all are working for the war, and the loss of a worker may well be more serious than the loss of a soldier'.[12]

It was absurd, therefore, simply to target those who wield arms and spare the men and women who, by their everyday work, make the use of arms possible. At the level of military ethics, it followed that the imperative could no longer be to cause the fewest possible civilian casualties, but rather to reduce the total number of victims to a minimum.

---

10   Ibid., 23 and 9.

11   Basil Liddell Hart, *Paris, or The Future of War*, New York: Dutton, 1925, 44, quoted in Satia, 'The Defence of Inhumanity', 36.

12   Giulio Douhet, 'La grande offensive aerea', *Scritti inediti*, Florence: Scuola di Guerra Aerea, 1951, 127.

If it is more effective to kill workers than to fire on enemy trenches, why not use an instrument that makes it possible to bring the conflict to an end more rapidly? Besides, had the naval blockade of the Great War not shown how it was impossible to distinguish between combatants and civilian population? In what way is it more 'humane' to starve to death rather than kill them with bombs?

It was in this way that the practice of targeting civilian populations, age-old in colonial wars, could in future be employed in Europe, and applied to peoples who had previously enjoyed an 'immunity'. How should we understand this extension of colonial practices to the whole of the world population? A comparison between air strategies in the colonial periphery and in Europe gives an answer that is both self-evident and disturbing: in both cases, war was the business of the whole people and no longer involved only the state, an entity transcending its citizens. In short, war became 'democratic'. For the moment, however, the British general staff undertook to 'preserve appearances ... by still nominally confining bombardment to targets which are strictly military ... to avoid emphasizing the truth that air warfare has made such restrictions obsolete and impossible'.[13] The restricted horizon of state-to-state war no longer existed; now it was whole peoples who made war and who, by the same token, became targets, whether directly or indirectly. This was how death in war was 'democratized', so that anyone at all could now be taken as a target.

National integration in Europe thus led to the paradoxical result that the modern European political form resembled in a certain respect the forms of tribal integration that had been attacked in Iraq. In both cases, these

---

13   Quoted by Satia, 'The Defence of Inhumanity', 42.

were wars in which the life of the population prevailed over the state: a war at a level beyond the state in Europe and a level below the state in the colonies. What Foucault called modern biopolitics was thus directly bound up with a 'thanatopolitics' of which the air arm constituted the most evident expression. Biopolitics and thanatopolitics were dialectically linked and targeted the same object: what biopolitics constructed, thanatopolitics sought to destroy. By so doing, this direct grip over the life and death of a people led to an important transformation in what is customarily called 'sovereignty'. European 'popular sovereignty' became increasingly similar to the forms of tribal integration that were attacked in the colonies.

The British general John Glubb explained as follows the difference, in his mind crucial for understanding Arab warfare, between 'rulers' and 'chiefs'. For the European mind, it was only a war waged by rulers that could be understood. A 'ruler' stands at the head of a political entity that transcends the individuals gathered into a 'people',[14] whereas a chief is immanent to his community: he does not act as a representative, but as a kind of emanation of his tribe. And this is why the doctrine of colonial war always emphasized the necessity of subjecting and chastising 'all refractory subjects'.[15] Colonial war was not a war against an overarching entity called 'government', but a rule against all and sundry. Colonial war was not waged against a transcendent body, but located in the strict immanence of politics.

It is precisely by this characteristic that colonial war provides the historical matrix for the evolution of warfare,

---

14   John Glubb, *The Story of the Arab Legion*, London: Hodder & Stoughton, 1948, chapter 'Arab Warfare', 117–31, particularly 118.

15   C. E. Callwell, *Small Wars: Their Principle and Practice*, ed. D. Porch, Lincoln: University of Nebraska Press, 1996, 41.

first of all in the European centre and then globally; and it was in terms of this characteristic that the return of Arthur Harris was premonitory. In Europe, it was customary to conceive war as a relation between states, and it was from this principle that the immunity of civilian populations followed. The revolutions of the end of the eighteenth century, however, placed the sovereign people at the centre of politics, and the contradictory principles of immunity and sovereignty were bound to create tensions. From this point of view, the First World War marked a watershed: the idea now came to prevail that war was fundamentally a relation of nation to nation, with the state being simply an emanation of a primordial entity that was the people united into a nation. Erich Ludendorff, chief of the German general staff during the First World War, wrote that 'it is in the people that the centre of gravity [of modern warfare] lies'.[16] It would thus be doubly illogical to spare civilians: not only do they count as much as soldiers in the war effort, but as citizens they collectively constitute the sovereign against whom war is waged.

Robert Brook-Popham, Harris's colleague in the colonial air force in Iraq before being appointed first head of the British air warfare school at Andover, accordingly declared in a lecture for RAF pilots: 'It is now the will power of the enemy nation that has to be broken, and to do this is the object of any nation that goes to war'.[17] The bomb dropped from a plane was thus the 'democratic' weapon

---

16 Erich Ludendorff, *Der totale Krieg*, Remscheid: Deutscher Militär Verlag, 1988, 28. (*The 'Total' War*, London: Friends of Europe, 1936.)

17 Robert Brooke-Popham, 'The Nature of War', lecture of 6 May 1925, UK Public Record Office, AIR 69/6, quoted Philip S. Meilinger, 'Trenchard and "Morale Bombing": The Evolution of Royal Air Force Doctrine Before Word War II', *Journal of Military History*, 60 (April 1996), 243–70.

par excellence, striking not simply the armed agents of a government, the 'paid gladiators' in Liddell Hart's phrase, but the sovereign itself. In other words, to target 'nations', civilian populations, the 'home front', did not just mean targeting the most vulnerable section of the enemy population. To take the people as target meant striking the political heart of the adversary. It meant targeting the real enemy rather than the epiphenomenon that was the state's military apparatus.

Bombing became 'democratic' in another sense as well. In a democracy, the population are not only an integral part of the national war effort; they are also responsible for the actions of their government. This explains the empirical fact that those political entities that we today refer to as 'democracies', and more particularly the representative democracies, were the ones to practise strategic bombing. Attacking the people was not just more effective, it was also more 'just'. Here again, it is amazing to note the parallels that exist between the evolution of war in Europe and in the colonies. The Arab populations, in particular, were proud, noble, independent, and free, living in a kind of 'primitive democracy', in which each individual naturally assumed responsibility for the whole community.[18] It followed that indiscriminately bombing a tribal population was a mark of respect for the indigenous culture.

If bombing pertains to a 'democratic' form of war, what concept of democracy are we dealing with here? It can hardly be in this context a regime of representative democracy – quite the contrary. The strategy of 'police bombing' defined the Iraqi or Afghan tribes as 'democratic' precisely because they did not practise representation. Each

---

18 John Slessor, *The Central Blue: The Autobiography of Sir John Slessor, Marshal of the RAF*, New York: Praeger, 1957, 54–5, and Satia, 'The Defence of Inhumanity', 37.

individual rather formed an organic part of the community. In the wake of Rousseau, doctrines of bombing conceived sovereignty as irreducible to representation. To speak of democracy in the case of Germany, the target of a projected strategic bombing offensive in 1918, and of an actual one during the Second World War, could seem equally incongruous.

More fundamentally, it is undeniable that the strategy of air bombing was necessarily based on a concept of the 'people' as the primordial political category. It was perhaps Trenchard who expressed this idea most clearly. In his tortuous formulation, the objective of air bombardment was to 'induce the enemy Government, by pressure from the population, to sue for peace, in exactly in the same way as starvation by blockading the country would force the Government to sue for peace.'[19] But if in Europe the aim of bombing was to compel a government to capitulate, the strategists did not explain the means by which they hoped to obtain this result. Would the enemy government listen to demands for peace formulated by the population? Would it capitulate for fear of revolt? Was it necessary to wait until a revolution had established a new government for the country to capitulate? Trenchard did not explain, no more than he explained how he conceived the relationship between governors and governed, or that of people and state.

We are faced here with a conceptual problem. We have no other concept available than that of democracy, a concept which – without having normative connotations – makes it possible to indicate the different active forms of political integration of the 'people', whether these are insurrectionary, parliamentary, monarchical-representative,

---

19   Quoted in Meilinger, 'Trenchard and "Morale Bombing"', 256.

plebiscitary, authoritarian, totalitarian, tribal, or other.[20] It is empirically indisputable, however, that strategic doctrines start from the idea that a public opinion 'influenced' by a campaign of strategic bombing will end up taking the political decision to capitulate. It is easy to see that this idea rests on a theory that mobilizes major concepts of political philosophy. And, far from being abstractions, these political concepts and theories were introduced into military doctrine and applied in the actual conduct of war. It is imperative therefore to investigate the political philosophy of the bomb. What conceptions of politics underpin it? What idea of the 'people' does it rest on? And what concept of democracy does it imply?

It is an unambiguous premise of bombing strategies that these forms of political integration have one fundamental thing in common: they are all 'democratic' in the minimal sense that the consent of the people is the ultimate source of all politics. 'Democracy' thus becomes something like a political a priori: even regimes that do not present democratic forms (such as the Arab tribes, or Nazism) are democratic in their essence. We need therefore to distinguish two concepts of democracy: democracy as form and democracy as essence.

If a strategy of bombing posits that all the social formations it takes as target are democratic in their essence, this clearly does not mean that they all have a democratic form. And if the form is not democratic, there is then a contradiction between form and essence. This leads either to a speculative teleology, according to which the 'normal' path for societies is to arrive at democracy, at the end of a long

---

20 Thomas Hippler, 'Krieg aus der Luft: Konzeptuelle Vorüberlegungen zur Entstehungsgeschichte des Bombenkrieges', in Wolfgang Hardtwig (ed.), *Ordnungen in der Krise. Zur politischen Kulturgeschichte 1900–1933*, Munich: Oldenbourg, 2007, 403–22.

and painful process, or else to a practical requirement for global politics: to act so that the different political regimes conform ever more with their democratic essence. In this way, political immanence generates a new transcendental instance, a global one this time, whose temporal register is a linear teleology.

Given this seemingly counter-intuitive use of the word 'democracy', a concept that has acquired crucial importance in the political field and consequently also in the field of war, some clarifications of its historical semantics are in order. For a very long time, 'democracy' was a pejorative concept, appealed to only by a small minority of revolutionary forces.[21] The founders of the US constitution still rejected it, which explains why the country became not a democracy but a 'constitutional republic'. It was only from the latter part of the nineteenth century that the concept began to acquire the status of a political a priori that it has maintained until today, and the First World War was a historical watershed also in this respect. Only one side, the Allied powers, ended up interpreting its struggle as a battle for democracy.

We should add right away that the concept long remained rather vague. For example, even at the start of the twentieth century, 'democracy' was not necessarily the opposite of 'dictatorship'; the two terms could even imply one another. Thus, the French officer corps, despite being gradually won to the republican cause,[22] fiercely opposed the 'famous and harmful legend of the revolutionary tradition' and openly supported a military-political leadership endowed with almost dictatorial power. Henri Mordacq,

---

21 See Luciano Canfora, *La Démocratie: histoire d'une idéologie*, Paris: Seuil, 2006.

22 Raoul Girardet, *La Société militaire de 1815 à nos jours*, Paris: Perrin, 1998, 121–44.

head of Clemenceau's private office and then minister of war, could write in 1912: 'Would this then be a *generalissimo*? Of course! In a democracy, still more so than in a monarchy, it is important in peacetime to ensure unity in the preparation for war, and in time of war, unity of command.'[23] This concept of democracy, which excluded neither dictatorial forms nor exceptional powers, may seem highly incongruous today, accustomed as we are to contrast democracy diametrically to 'totalitarianism'. Historically, however, there is nothing obvious about this meaning: to cite only one example, 'despotism' was, for the whole counter-revolutionary tradition, the logical and inevitable outcome of 'democracy'.

If, in the early twentieth century, 'democracy' was still sometimes close to 'totalitarian' forms, it was certainly always opposed to the monarchical principle. Though it seems indisputable today that Belgium and Spain are democracies, it was still hard at that time to envisage a democracy within a monarchical setting. The British, for example, being themselves the subjects of a king, preferred to present the war as a battle for 'Law, Justice, Responsibility, Liberty, Citizenship', concepts that 'are free to be the attributes of any race or any nation. They belong to civilized humanity as a whole'.[24] In 1914, therefore, the words 'liberty', 'law', 'justice', 'parliamentarism', and 'citizenship' were not yet crystallized in a concept of democracy that embraced them all. The dominant concept was not yet that of democracy but rather that of 'civilization'.

In France, the fragile union of republicans and Catholics

---

23 Commandant Mordacq (École supérieure de la guerre), *Politique et stratégie dans une démocratie*, Paris: Plon, 1912, 259 and 266.

24 Alfred Zimmern, 'German Culture and the British Commonwealth', in R. W. Seton-Watson, J. Dover Wilson, Alfred E. Zimmern, and Arthur Greenwood (eds), *The War and Democracy*, London: Macmillan, 1915, 364.

suggested a certain conceptual prudence. Henri Bergson, for example, one of the leading ideologists of the war, mobilized a whole arsenal of classical antagonisms (civilization/barbarism, law/force, liberty/mechanism, spirituality/materiality, moral force/material force, sincerity/artifice, humanity/militarism, etc.), but assiduously avoided the term 'democracy'.[25] And paradoxically, a book published by Oxford professors in 1915, despite being titled *The War and Democracy*, refers almost exclusively to 'civilization' and scarcely at all to democracy, despite stating that

> Democracy is not a mere form of government. It does not depend on ballot boxes or franchise laws or any constitutional machinery. These are but its trappings. Democracy is a spirit and an atmosphere, and its essence is trust in the moral instincts of the people.[26]

In short, we are dealing with a concept of democracy that is minimal and very vague. In 1914, civilization remained the really key concept. It would only be dethroned by global 'democracy' in the inter-war years, when its too openly colonial connotations began to seem embarrassing. The same process of conceptual substitution was effected in the field of aviation: the bomber, originally a weapon of civilization, became a weapon of democracy.

These political values, far from being universally shared, were arranged according to respective geopolitical positions. The 'geopolitics of values' followed closely the distribution of power on the world scale, and it was the hegemonic powers in particular that appealed to civilization,

25 The word is actually absent in Bergson's wartime interventions, collected in Henri Bergson, *La Signification de la guerre*, Paris: Bloud et Gay, 2015.
26 Seton-Watson, Dover Wilson, Zimmern and Greenwood (eds), *The War and Democracy*, 1.

then gradually to democracy. The contenders, on the other hand, often rejected these terms, or at least sought to reappropriate them by altering their meaning. Two flagrant examples of the second strategy can be given. During the Cold War, the Soviet contender tried to undo the opposition between democracy and totalitarianism by distinguishing 'real democracy' from 'formal democracy'; and during the First World War, the German contender rejected the concept of civilization and preferred that of *Kultur*.[27] There were several reasons for these divergences. But instead of seeking these in remote history, in the specificities of different 'national cultures', or in some *Sonderweg*, we need only underline the most obvious aspect: the position of the different countries in the world system.

If each nation develops an image of itself, its combat, and its differences with enemy nations, this clearly does not mean that war is no more than a confrontation of national egoisms that are basically equivalent. On the contrary, all nations fight for causes with a universal claim.[28] The universalization of causes is even a key element in the totalization of war. The fight is no longer for limited political objectives, but for causes that are inherently just and that invest nations with a mission that is more than their own, a mission for humanity, a universal mission. From this point, there is no longer any right to lose a war; rather, the moral duty of victory in order to preserve, in the name of humanity, the universal values of which one's own nation is the bearer.

---

27 Jörg Fisch, 'Zivilisation, Kultur', in Otto Brunner, Werner Conze, and Reinhart Koselleck (ed.), *Geschichtliche Grundbegriffe. Historisches Lexikon zur politisch-sozialen Sprache in Deutschland*, Stuttgart: Klett-Cotta, 1978, vol. 7, 679–774.

28 See Hew Strachan, *The First World War, Volume 1: 'To Arms'*, Oxford: Oxford University Press, 2001, chapter 'The Ideas of 1914', 1114–39.

According to the universalism of the 'Lockean' hegemon, war was a battle of democracy, liberalism, the rights of peoples, and, ultimately, of civilization, against militarism, the right of the strongest, collectivism, and statolatry.[29] Initially, the German war ideology was not so different from that of the French and British: Germany was fighting against despotism and barbarism, two enemies traditionally associated with the 'Asiatic' character embodied by Russia. This is how the Swedish socialist Gustaf Steffen justified Germany's entry into the war: 'The religion of Muscovite imperialism is primitive, medieval, literally semi-barbaric … Its perception of law, as well as its morals and its social sentiment, indicate not a European type but a backward type of Western and Central Asia.'[30]

The alliance of the Western powers with Russia forced the Central Powers to refine their ideological arsenal and give greater emphasis to the typical 'Hobbesian' perspective of contenders. The democratic and liberal ideals proclaimed by the hegemon were denounced as the ideological camouflage of capitalist egoism, colonial exploitation, and imperialism in all its forms. Gustaf Steffen could then write that 'the alliance of France and Great Britain with Russia against Germany and Austria-Hungary is therefore an alliance … against the vital and indivisible interests of Europe as a whole.'[31] At the risk of extreme simplification, the structuring dichotomy ('civilization' versus *Kultur*) presented an opposition between the 'unitary' universalism of the hegemony and the 'culturalist' universalism of the

---

29 Martha Hanna, *The Mobilization of Intellect: French Scholars and Writers during the Great War*, Cambridge, MA: Harvard University Press, 1996, 108–18.

30 Gustaf Steffen, *Weltkrieg und Imperialismus. Sozialpsychologische Dokumente und Beobachtungen vom Weltkrieg 1914–15*, Jena: Diederichs, 1915, 49.

31 Ibid., 51.

contender, an opposition that is found in several other contexts through to today. Civilization is one, measured only by advances and delays. Cultures, on the other hand, are intrinsically different and bound to remain so.

The First World War marked a break in this respect. Initially, the notions of civilization and culture had the same meaning, denoting the historicity of human action. The former was more usual in the French- and English-speaking worlds, the second in the German-speaking lands. These words, invented in the second half of the eighteenth century, were initially used only in the singular.[32] The plural came to prominence in the Germanic space, responding to a need to conceptualize the specificity of German culture as opposed to the dominant culture of France. On the other hand, since France represented the most advanced degree of civilization (in the singular), the question of the specificity of its culture quite simply did not arise.

With the First World War, what had been synonymous terms suddenly acquired opposing meanings that efforts were made to spell out. Thus, according to the journalist Jacques Bainville, close to Action Française, 'German *Kultur* is simply a form of barbarism'. Whereas the concepts of *Kultur* and civilization both implied a linear historical process, their disassociation made historical retreat conceivable. This was clearly the case with Russia after the October Revolution, and also the case with Germany, which fell back from civilization into barbarism.[33] The

---

32 See Fisch, 'Zivilisation, Kultur'.

33 In the words of Walter Benjamin, 'the current amazement that the things we are experiencing are "still" possible in the twentieth century is *not* philosophical. This amazement is not the beginning of knowledge – unless it is the knowledge that the view of history which gives rise to it is untenable.' *Selected Writings: 1938–1940, Volume 4*, Cambridge, MA: Belknap Press of Harvard University Press, 2003, 392.

reason for this was that one side of German *Kultur* – the bad, 'Hegelian' side – gained the upper hand over the good side, that embodied by Kant.[34] Air warfare was a flagrant example of this. As a colonial air commander in Iraq, Arthur Harris had explained that these savage Arabs and Kurds

> now knew what a real bombardment is, they understood the human and material damage it can do; they know now that in 45 minutes an entire village ... can be practically wiped off the map, that a third of its inhabitants can be killed or injured by three or four aircraft that do not present them either with real targets, or with the possibility of warlike bravery, or with an effective means of escaping.[35]

After having coordinated the 'fire storms' of Bomber Command during the Second World War, Harris revisited his experience of colonial bombing, to say that 'In this, as in all the RAF's many operations over *savage countries, including Germany,* capture by the natives was one of the worst things we had to fear.'[36]

Once again, these ideologies are inseparable from their geopolitical situations, the different strategic orientations, and their evolution in the course of the war. German 'culturalism' was thus in phase with the German strategy on a global scale, which consisted in globalizing the conflict and banking on anticolonial revolts, and particularly on pan-Slavic movements, but also on nationalisms of all kinds (Jewish, Irish, Polish, Finnish, Estonian, Lithuanian,

34 On the dichotomy between 'Hegelian' and 'Kantian' in Germany, see Hanna, *The Mobilization of Intellect*, 106–41.

35 Quoted by David Omissi, *Air Power and Colonial Control: The Royal Air Force 1919–1939*, Manchester: Manchester University Press, 1990, 154.

36 Harris, *Bomber Offensive*, 20. Emphasis added.

Ukrainian, Georgian), in order to deprive its adversaries of their imperial resources.[37] This support provided to different nationalisms and revolutionary movements did not necessarily have the aim of creating German domination, and could be completely sincere.[38] Thus the Kaiser wrote in a letter,

> It has long been ... my wish to see the Mohammedan nations independent and to achieve for their states the maximum of free development. I am therefore not only immediately concerned to help the Mohammedan people in their struggle for independence, but I will support them in the future through My Imperial Government ... The community of interests which exists today between the German people and the Mohammedans will continue in being after the end of the war.[39]

He accordingly exhorted German diplomats and agents to

> inflame the Muslim world so that it rebels against this nation of shopkeepers, hateful, dishonest and devoid of principles ... From now on, we must implacably denounce this whole structure, publicly tear to pieces the mask of Christian peace it presents, and nail the pharisaic hypocrisy of peace to the pillory.[40]

Since anticolonial ideology was an integral part of German strategy, it is not surprising that Erich Ludendorff

---

37 Hew Strachan, *The First World War*, chapter 'Germany's Global Strategy', especially 696.

38 Even Fritz Fischer concedes this point. See *Germany's Aims in the First World War*, New York: Norton, 1968, 120.

39 Ibid.

40 Quoted in Ulrich Gehrke, *Persien in der deutschen Orientpolitik während des Ersten Weltkrieges*, Stuttgart: Kohlhammer, 1960, vol. 1, 1.

explicitly saw a parallel between colonial war and the 'total war' that he called for:

> The days of Cabinet wars and of wars with limited political aims belong to a bygone age. Such wars were marauding and predatory expeditions, rather than morally justified combats, as is a total war, for the preservation of the nation. Colonial wars, wherein nations or tribes are fighting only for their life, and whom the opponents can simply crush, bear, as far as the attacked nations or tribes are concerned, the character of a total war, and are waged by such tribes for moral reasons. For the rest, these wars are most immoral actions, and do not deserve the sublime and serious definition of warfare.[41]

The geostrategic and ideological developments that took place during the First World War largely explain why the idea of an air force with a cosmopolitan reach was taken up by the Western powers, the winners of the Great War, rather than in other parts of the world. Added to this is the fact that a clause of the Versailles Treaty obliged Germany, still powerful though seriously weakened, to renounce air war – a clause that was not respected, however, since the new Soviet contender put at Germany's disposal the air base of Lipezk as a secret training facility for its pilots.[42] The Soviet Union itself, despite steadily moving up to the rank of a new contender, was still occupied with consolidating its power domestically and emerging from an agricultural economy. It was thus quite naturally the Western powers that took on the task of guaranteeing the world order. In this context, the realization of a cosmopolitan air force acquired unprecedented urgency: Europe was

---

41 Erich Ludendorff, *The 'Total' War*, 16–17. Translation modified.
42 Hanfried Schliephake, *The Birth of the Luftwaffe*, London: Ian Allan, 1971, 9–21.

itself in the process of becoming the theatre of a confrontation between the forces of good and evil, with certain nations losing their 'civilized' status. No other technology than aviation could embody the new transcendental instance on the world scale, becoming its executive organ, its sword of vengeance, its justice.

In France, the author of a doctoral thesis in political science could thus emphasize the cosmopolitical aspects of air power, the use of the air arm during the First World War having demonstrated 'the necessity of adapting old rules by all civilized states, acting in agreement as members of a single union and committing themselves to ensuring the application of these'.[43] If it is obvious that the bombed insurgents in the colonies were not members of this club, the author does not say which states did count among the 'civilized'. In Great Britain, one of the leading theorist of air war, the top civil servant James Molony Spaight, put forward remarkably similar arguments: '[Air power must be] envisaged as a disarming, a preventive, a war-breaking rather than a war-making force. For that reason it commends itself as the ideal instrument for use in the "sanction wars" of the future.'

Aviation thus marked the end of 'private wars', a category that embraced all classic inter-state conflicts. Air war, on the other hand, heralded the age of world peace. 'Private war, except in self-defence, is outlawed. The next step may be the creation of a procedure and machinery of enforcement of that outlawry.'[44] The future that Spaight wrote about would thus be an age of world peace, effective peace, a peace organized and defended. As a realist, however, the

43 Émile Lebon, *De la Guerre aérienne dans ses rapports avec le droit international (la leçon des faits)*, doctoral thesis, Université de Nancy, 1923, 223.

44 James M. Spaight, *Air Power and the Cities*, London: Longmans, Green and Co., 1930, vi–vii.

British civil servant recognized that the international order would never be perfect, even if it took the federal form of a United States of Europe. No one could exclude 'the possibility of a failure or refusal on the part of an individual state or of a coalition of states to fulfil [its commitments]'. As a consequence, means of coercion had to be available in order to deter potential contenders in the world arena.

More surprising, perhaps, Ernest Seillière, philosopher, member of the Académie, theorist of imperialism and close to the 'revolutionary right', also became an apologist for this kind of cosmopolitical pacifism, declaring in 1925 that the possibilities opened up by air war necessitated 'the constitution of a solid international gendarmerie, with both a preventive and a repressive role, with the most civilized nations providing its elements and having its costs paid, as far as possible, by those who provoke its deployment.'[45] In the United States, Clifford Harmon, president of the International Air League, advanced similar proposals, suggesting the creation of an international air force placed under the aegis of the League of Nations.[46] Under the name of the 'Silver Wings of Peace', this international air force would be made up of the world's best pilots, both men and women. In the event of an international crisis, its planes would drop leaflets on the countries concerned before bombing them.[47] As we can see, even in their least details these pacifist fantasies were perfectly in tune with the RAF regulations for police bombing in Iraq and Afghanistan.

---

45 In a collective work edited by André Henry-Coüannier, *Légitimité de la guerre aérienne*, Paris: Per Orbem, 1925, 5.

46 Quoted by Italo Balbo, *Realtà e metodo dell'aeronautica italiana*, '*Discorso pronunciato alla camera dei deputati sul Bilancio dell'aeronautica l'11 giugno 1929*', Rome: Tipografia della camera dei deputati, 1929, 42.

47 Joseph J. Corn, The *Winged Gospel: America's Romance with Aviation*, Baltimore: Johns Hopkins University Press, 2001, 59.

CHAPTER 6

People and Populace

Ever since Christmas he had felt tired, sad, empty, to the point that his doctor had strongly advised him to take a month's holiday. But important business kept him at work; he had responsibilities and the situation was hard to manage – very hard indeed. Every morning, the sense of duty and the hope of improving things pressed him to his office, but each evening he could not help but realize that his efforts had met with renewed defeat. At the end of his forces, he began to write to his London friend, the feminist Alice Clark, one of his letters, brief and luminous 'like visits from angels', to tell her of the troubles inflicting him.[1]

Jan Smuts was on the point of becoming prime minister of South Africa. A decorated Afrikaner commander in the Second Boer War, he had harassed the British by employing a perfected and uncommonly violent tactic of hit and run. Yet he had been forced to concede defeat and negotiate peace, after 'more than 20,000 women and children [had] already perished in the enemy's concentration camps'.[2] As one of the artisans of South African unity achieved in 1910, he simultaneously headed the Ministries of the Interior,

1 Letter from Jan Smuts to Alice Clark, Cape Town, 24 March 1922, in Jean van der Poel (ed.), *Selections from the Smuts Papers, vol. 5* (September 1919–November 1934), Cambridge: Cambridge University Press, 1973, 114–15.

2 Smuts' speech at Vereeniging, 30 May 1902, in W. Hancock and Jean van der Poel (ed.), *Selections from the Smuts Papers, vol. 1* (June 1886–May 1902), Cambridge: Cambridge University Press, 1966, 527.

Mines, and Defence, before commanding in the First World War the South African force that attacked the German colonies of South-West Africa (present-day Namibia) and then East Africa (now Burundi, Rwanda, and part of Tanzania). Appointed to the Imperial War Cabinet in London, he submitted in 1917 his famous report on 'Air Organization and the Direction of Aerial Operations', considered the 'Magna Carta' of air power. This resulted in the creation of the Royal Air Force, the first independent air army, designed to protect British territories in a near future in which

> aerial operations with their devastation of enemy lands and destruction of industrial and populous centers on a vast scale may become the principal operations of war, to which the older forms of military and naval operations may become secondary and subordinate.[3]

Smuts was, in other words, one of the leading institutional architects of the aerial bombing to come.

Despite this, he was convinced that it was preferable to avoid a new war. The best means of achieving this was to seek a reconciliation with Germany: at the Versailles conference, Smuts vigorously opposed the French delegation, which was far from sharing his opinion.[4] Of cosmopolitical views, he championed the creation of a League of Nations shaped according to the model of the

---

3 *Air Force Magazine*, 92/1 (January 2009), http://airforcemag. com/MagazineArchive/Pages/2009/January%202009/0109keeperfile. aspx (accessed 24 May 2013).

4 Mark Mazower, *No Enchanted Palace: The End of Empire and the Ideological Origins of the United Nations*, Princeton: Princeton University Press, 2009, Chapter 1, 'Jan Smuts and Imperial Internationalism', 28–65. See also the classic work by Arno J. Mayer, *Politics and Diplomacy of Peacemaking: Containment and Counterrevolution at Versailles, 1918–1919*, London: Weidenfeld & Nicolson, 1967.

British Commonwealth, so that peace should be 'founded in human ideals, in principles of freedom and equality'.[5] In future, any party which disturbed this peace would be stripped of the rights traditionally attaching to war and 'treated as the common criminal that it is'.[6] Preparing British forces for strategic bombing while supporting a rapprochement of peoples within the League of Nations, Smuts was a perfect representative of the cosmopolitism of the bombers that was in the process of coming into being.

On return to his native South Africa, he had to face other challenges. Already in 1914, he had not hesitated to declare martial law in the face of a general strike, and to deport its leaders without any form of trial – a decision, to put it politely, on the border of legality. After the First World War, the situation grew still worse: encouraged by anticolonial and Communist uprisings, black workers began to organize in a 'federation of labour', the African People's Organization. The threat was serious. Smuts declared before the South African parliament that in this country, 'a small white colony in a Dark Continent', it was imperative that 'the white people must ever be watchful and careful, and highly organized and ready to put down with an iron hand all attempts' at subversion.[7] Faced with this double threat, of both race and class, he asked London to help him by sending a military plane and pilot, not without guaranteeing the imperial authorities that 'the machine will not be used against the white population of Johannesburg but will be held in reserve mainly for demonstration purposes and consequent moral effect

---

5   J. C. Smuts, *The League of Nations: A Practical Suggestion* (1919), 14.

6   Ibid., 62.

7   Quoted by W. K. Hancock, *Smuts I: The Sanguine Years 1870–1919*, Cambridge: Cambridge University Press, 1962, 369.

against the natives on the Reef should they become out of hand.'[8]

Despite this determination, things continued to grow worse. If it was not surprising that the blacks, these 'children of nature', were inclined to violent insurrection, the gangrene was now affecting the white working class: a South African Communist Party was founded in 1921; at the same time, a strike of (white) miners degenerated to become a serious revolutionary threat.[9] Thus, against all his instincts, Smuts found himself compelled to transgress the taboo, to go back on the promise he had made in 1919, and above all to betray his segregationist beliefs. He ordered the air arm to be used against the strikers.[10] Despite being Communists, these were still white. The misfortune had plumbed its depths.

Smuts, inspired only by 'considerations of humanity and benevolent sentiments towards the workers', was treated as a 'butcher and executioner' by the white insurgents who, being themselves deeply racist, accused him even of betraying the cause of 'white South Africa'.[11] It is easy to understand why in this month of March 1922, Smuts fell into depression. A short time later, he withdrew from political life to devote himself to teaching, philosophy, and

---

8   Quoted in David Killingray, '"A Swift Agent of Government":
Air Power in British Colonial Africa, 1916–1939', *Journal of African History*, 25 (1984), 432.

9   W. K. Hancock, *Smuts II: The Fields of Force, 1919–1950*, Cambridge: Cambridge University Press, 1968, 62–88.

10   Townshend, '"A Swift Agent of Government"', 432.

11   The author of a biography of William Andrews, first president of the South African Communist Party, explained in 1943 that the strikers' slogan 'for a White South Africa', although it 'appears reactionary on the surface ... was nevertheless founded on sound working-class instinct': it served as a 'defence against capitalist aggression' (R. K. Cope, *Comrade Bill: The Life and Times of W. H. Andrews, Workers' Leader*, Cape Town: Stewart Printing, 1943, 231).

the writing of his major work, *Holism and Evolution*, published in 1926. For the moment, he accepted responsibility for his decision, in the belief that he had had no choice but to act as he had done:

> So that society does not fall into ruins, it must rest on the firm assurance that force will be used. It will remain so as long as human nature has not undergone a profound change. As in Russia, so elsewhere, the danger is that in a very short time the slow results of ages of progress may be undone.[12]

The 'global civil war' that had begun with the First World War shattered the old division of the world between a centre in which violence was limited by the state and a periphery in which it could be total. As we have seen, the bombing of civilian populations in the periphery was justified by the colonies' lack of civilization. This argument would now be applied to certain categories of Europeans as well. By proposing a strategic air offensive against Germany in 1918, an offensive indissociable from the justification of a war for 'civilization', Smuts contributed to opening the door to this development. Since Germany was despite everything a European state, the idea of using the air arm against it was still embarrassing. The world configuration created by the October Revolution added a supplementary dimension: the looming threat to civilization no longer necessarily came just from outside.

From the month of December 1917, thus immediately after the Bolshevik revolution, the British authorities used air power to intimidate strikers in Coventry and exhort them to return to work with leaflets dropped by plane. The

---

12 Letter to Alice Clark of 24 March 1922, in van der Poel (ed.), *Selection from the Smuts Papers, vol. 1*, 115.

wartime strikes seriously worried the government: would the population hold firm? Was the country to be paralysed by a mass panic? And, still more important, would British workers imitate the Russian example? Worries about a threat of revolution even came to overshadow the confrontation in the trenches. In his *War Memoirs*, British Prime Minister David Lloyd George wrote this striking passage: 'the contentment and co-operation of the wage-earners was our vital concern, and industrial unrest spelt a graver menace to our endurance and ultimate victory than even the military strength of Germany.'[13]

In the wake of the Great War, Great Britain was probably closer to revolution than it had ever been in its recent history. Conscripts of working-class origin who had survived the horrors of the trenches were far less inclined to accept the poverty or unemployment that awaited them on return. The fact that the Central Powers had collapsed at the end of the war demonstrated that a radical change was possible. The whole of Europe was shaken by a revolutionary wave – from Petrograd to Berlin and Turin. Rather than continue the war to German capitulation, the Western leaders preferred a rapid armistice. On 9 November 1918, the head of the British imperial general staff, Henry Wilson, described this scene in his diary:

> Cabinet 6.30 to 8 p.m. Lloyd George read two wires from Tiger [Clemenceau] describing Foch's interviews with the Boches, and Tiger is afraid that Germany will break up and Bolshevism become rampant. Lloyd George asked me if I wanted this, or would rather have an armistice, and I unhesitatingly said 'armistice'. All the cabinet agreed ... Wires came in during the Cabinet to say Kaiser and Crown

---

13 David Lloyd George, *War Memoirs*, London: Nicholson & Watson, 1934, vol. 4, 1925–6.

Prince had escaped to Holland, and German towns were in the hands of Revolutionaries.[14]

Clemenceau did indeed fear a German collapse. There was now a visible enemy that was still more threatening: 'Our real danger now is not the Boches but Bolshevism', General Wilson summed up.[15]

On 10 November 1918, Churchill outlined the consequences of the new situation: 'We might have to build up the German Army, as it was important to get Germany on her legs again, for fear of the spread of Bolshevism.'[16] Ferdinand Foch even sketched plans for an offensive against the Bolsheviks to be conducted jointly by French, American, and German troops. The Social-Democratic coalition of Ebert and Noske, backed by the remains of the German military apparatus, would be enough not only to eliminate the Spartacist revolution but also, at the same stroke, a good part of the Social-Democratic support as well.[17] As we know, this decisive weakening of the German workers' movement would be one of the factors that made possible the rise of fascism. On the other hand, it was imperative to intervene in Russia, the new epicentre of the world Communist threat, where the revolution was in the process of consolidating itself – particularly thanks to Germany's 'revolutionary strategy' and the decision to

---

14 Quoted by C. E. Callwell, *Field Marshal Sir Henry Wilson: His Life and Diaries*, London: Cassell, 1927, vol. 1, 148.

15 Quoted ibid., and Keith Jeffery, *Field Marshal Sir Henry Wilson: A Political Soldier*, Oxford: Oxford University Press, 2006, 229.

16 Quoted by Martin Gilbert, 'The Origins of the "Iron Curtain" Speech', in R. Crosby Kemper III (ed.), *Winston Churchill: Resolution, Defiance, Magnanimity, Good Will*, Columbia: University of Missouri Press, 1996, 37.

17 See Sebastian Haffner, *Failure of a Revolution: Germany 1918–1919*, New York: Library Press, 1973.

return Lenin and the Bolsheviks from their Swiss exile, a decision that was sealed by the ephemeral peace of Brest-Litovsk and the similarly ephemeral German annexation of a territory stretching from Estonia to the Black Sea.

The Allied intervention in the Russian civil war began in 1918 and mobilized troops from fourteen countries.[18] While the use of poison gas by the Germans in 1915 had provoked indignation from the Western powers, the British had no hesitation in dropping chemical bombs on Russia. Churchill had already declared himself 'strongly favourable to the use of poison gas against barbarian tribes'.[19] Chemical weapons, moreover, were 'the right medicine for the Bolshevist'.[20] Nor did the Red Army hesitate to use this type of weapon, for example against the Tambov peasant revolt in 1921.[21] The 'barbarians', those who could legitimately be bombed, machine-gunned, and gassed from the air, were no longer necessarily 'noble savages' living in remote and exotic climes. The threat had now become still more serious: insidious, with a white face, approaching the centre to devour it.

The Communist threat was advancing, and the anticolonial struggle also came nearer home. In January 1919 the Irish war of independence broke out, and the insurgents harassed the British army using guerrilla methods. The viceroy, Lord French, banked on the air control that was

18 Clifford Kinvig, *Churchill's Crusade: The British Invasion of Russia, 1918–1920*, London: Hambledon Continuum, 2006.

19 'Winston S. Churchill: departmental minute (Churchill papers 16/16), 12 May 1919', in Martin Gilbert, *Winston S. Churchill*, London: Heinemann, 1976, vol. 4, companion, part 1, *Documents January 1917–June 1919*, 649.

20 Simon Jones, '"The Right Medicine for the Bolshevist": British Air-Dropped Chemical Weapons in North Russia, 1919', *Imperial War Museum Review*, 12 (1999), 78–88.

21 Stéphane Courtois et al., *The Black Book of Communism*, Cambridge, MA: Harvard University Press, 1988, 116–17.

being developed in the overseas colonies: aircraft equipped
with bombs and machine guns would 'put the fear of God
into these playful young Sinn Feiners'. In London, caution
was the word, fearing 'the great risk of death and injury
to innocent people, owing to the extreme difficulty of distinguishing innocent from guilty from an aeroplane'.[22]
General Neville Macready, commander of the British
troops in Ireland, continued nonetheless to ask permis-
sion to use bombers in the case that rebels could be 'clearly
distinguished', the ubiquity of aircraft being the obvious
solution in the face of the guerrilla fighters' mobility, which
otherwise gave them a decisive advantage. The government
finally gave in: in March 1921, it authorized the use of
aircraft, but only in rural zones and against units actually
engaged in combat or actively preparing this.[23] As in 1918,
however, the decision came too late. The ceasefire declared
in July made it impossible for the air arm to deploy its full
potential.

The 'Celtic fringe' of the British Isles, however, never
enjoyed the same status as the real centre, England. It is
far more significant that English territory could itself
become a target for counter-revolutionary aviation. In
1920, the Minister of Transport believed a revolution
on English soil was imminent; and, in a text of counter-
insurrectionary strategy, Hugh Trenchard, head of RAF
general staff, now defined the role that aircraft would play
in the repression of a coming civil war. Although aircraft
were 'at present an inaccurate weapon', whose use in an
urban environment involved serious risks, he recommended

---

22 Charles Townshend, *The British Campaign in Ireland, 1919–1921: The Development of Political and Military Policies*, Oxford: Oxford University Press, 1975, 170–1.
23 David Omissi, *Air Power and Colonial Control: The Royal Air Force 1919–1939*, Manchester: Manchester University Press, 1990, 43.

using 'a limited amount of bombing and machine-gun fire' against cities held by rebels, and 'where a majority of the inhabitants are definitely hostile' to the political system.[24]

Fearing that this could provoke outrage in public opinion, Churchill demanded the suppression of any reference to England in written communications. He did, however, approve a later version of the text, which provided that aircraft would only be used in Great Britain in case of war, or in the improbable case that rioters themselves used aeroplanes. In conformity with this arrangement, the Royal Air Force ensured the distribution of Conservative newspapers in all British cities during the general strike of 1926, and would equally serve to ferry blacklegs to work in factories on strike, manage infrastructure, and arrest 'prominent Communists'. England, perceived as a haven of peace in the old world system, itself became the potential theatre of a type of violence previously confined to the periphery. From now on, insurgents, rebels, Communists, all elements susceptible of destabilizing the bourgeois and imperialist social order, were equated with the barbarians who could legitimately be subjected to bombing. By the same token, the old spatial separation between the centre (space of peace and law) and the periphery (space of war and violence) tended to disappear. The border between interior and exterior was no longer necessarily a geographical one.

This gave a greater complexity to the 'democratic' character of the air force and illustrated in return certain aspects of national integration in the European countries. In the lectures he delivered at the British school of air warfare at Andover, Robert Brook-Popham cited 'democratization', 'industrialization', and 'trade unionism' as the three decisive factors that had led to a closer integration

---

24   Ibid., 41. The following paragraph is based on pages 39–43 of this book.

of 'the people' into the war effort. From now on, the distinction between combatants and non-combatants was de facto obsolete.[25] If the whole people could be subjected to bombing, it was equally true that, to paraphrase Orwell, some were more 'people' than others. Class difference was one of the cornerstones of air strategy. This is perhaps the red thread that would subsequently run through all future strategies of air war in Europe. If each person became a potential target, it was workers who were targeted above all. The reason for this was that the working-class population concentrated the three factors that, according to Brook-Popham, tied the people to modern war: as citizens of 'democratic' states, they not only ran the industries, but also had the possibility of halting production by strike or revolt.

By the revolutionary threat that they embodied, the working-class population found themselves logically in the firing line of the bombers. They were even targeted from two sides: by counter-revolutionary aviation on the part of their own government, and by the bombers of the 'enemy nation' on the other. In Europe, the working-class population thus became the lynchpin of bomber strategy. This was guided by the idea that this class, as the key segment of the war effort, was at the same time the least politically integrated section of the population. Industrialization, the specific strength of European nations, was based on the existence of a working class, and thus on a constant threat to the social order. The foundations of this order were intrinsically unstable.

---

25   Robert Brooke-Popham, 'The Nature of War', lecture of 6 May 1925, Public Record Office, Kew, AIR 69/6, quoted by Philip S. Meilinger, 'Trenchard and "Morale Bombing": The Evolution of Royal Air Force Doctrine Before Word War II', *Journal of Military History*, 60 (April 1996), 243–70.

Air war is essentially democratic, inasmuch as the 'people' constitute the primordial political entity for it. But if war becomes the business of the 'people', the fact of targeting workers reveals a constitutive ambiguity: what 'people' are to be bombed? The collective sovereign, or rather the 'populace'? This uncertainty is revealing in itself.

The most striking illustration of this double nature of the 'people' is perhaps found in H. G. Wells's *The War in the Air*, which, when it was published in 1908, had a deep influence on the Western public, particularly on military theorists, who often quoted it.[26] Summed up very briefly, its plot goes as follows: In a war against the United States, the German air force bombs New York with Zeppelins before being defeated by Chinese and Japanese aviation. There follows an economic crash, a global 'Muslim insurrection', and the collapse of all organized social life.

In the bombed New York of Wells's novel,

> the airships ... smashed up the city as a child will shatter its cities of brick and card. Below, they left ruins and blazing conflagrations and heaped and scattered dead; men, women, and children mixed together as though they had been no more than Moors, or Zulus, or Chinese.[27]

What did the New Yorkers have in common with these 'savages'? The fact that they could be bombed and their corpses piled up, of course, but also and above all, that air bombing rendered the established power of the state inoperative: when the American authorities decide to

---

26 See Robert Wohl, *A Passion for Wings: Aviation and the Western Imagination 1908–1914*, Yale University Press, 1994, 70–1 and Samuel Hynes, *The Soldiers' Tale: Bearing Witness to a Modern War*, New York: Allen Lane, 1997, 81.

27 H. G. Wells, *The War in the Air*, in *The Atlantic edition*, vol. 20, London: Fisher, 1926, 207.

capitulate after the German bombing, the people launch a struggle for national independence. Despite its tremendous power of destruction, the air arm is incapable of controlling territory: 'The Germans had struck at the head, and the head was conquered and stunned – only to release the body from its rule. New York had become a headless monster, no longer capable of collective submission.'[28]

Bombing thus brings to light the democratic paradox of the inadequacy between constituted power and constituent power.[29] The people take matters into their own hands, appropriate the collective power, and wage a democratic war. With admirable clairvoyance, Wells showed back in 1908 that the connection between democracy and modern warfare, of which air bombing is the symptomatic expression, is far more complex than today's theorists of 'democratic peace' would like to believe. The political 'head', the constituted power, certainly recognizes the necessity of capitulating under the bombs, but the 'body' of society, led by blind impulses, launches a movement of national and popular resistance, what Clausewitz called a *Volkskrieg*. According to Wells, the fundamental paradox of the age lay precisely in the contradiction between the technical necessities of war, on the one hand, and democratic participation, on the other.[30] Incapable of containing popular insurrection, aviation displayed this political paradox:

> The special peculiarities of aerial warfare were of such a nature as to trend, once it had begun, almost inevitable towards social disorganization ... the immense power of destruction an airship has over the thing below, and its

---

28 Ibid., 202.
29 Chantal Mouffe, *The Democratic Paradox*, London: Verso, 2000.
30 Wells, *The War in the Air*, 181–2.

relative inability to occupy or police or guard or garrison a surrendered position. Necessarily, in the face of urban populations in a state of economic disorganization and infuriated and starving, this led to violent and destructive collisions, and even where the air-fleet floated inactive above, there would be civil conflict and passionate disorder below. Nothing, comparable to this state of affairs had been known in the previous history of warfare, unless we take such as case as that of a nineteenth-century warship attacking some large savage or barbaric settlement, or one of those naval bombardments that disfigure the history of Great Britain in the late eighteenth century. Then, indeed, there had been cruelties and destruction that faintly foreshadowed the horrors of the aerial war. Moreover, before the twentieth century the world had had but one experience, and that a comparatively light one, in the Communist insurrection of Paris, 1871, of the possibilities of a modern urban population under warlike stress.[31]

The most advanced weapon of its time thus undermined the very conditions of its superiority: it returned modern society, complex and highly differentiated, to the 'savage and barbarian' state in which the colonies remained, and to which Communist insurrections also threatened to reduce us to. Once the state was destroyed by bombs and had become incapable of guaranteeing the bourgeois social order, New Yorkers were transformed into 'savages', comparable to the barbarians of the colonies. Here the two meanings of the notion 'people' come together: it is precisely the savage 'populace' that seizes sovereignty amid the ruins of the state and bourgeois civil society.

We can now see more clearly the point of the political edifice that bombing is supposed to explode. Its aim is to

31   Ibid., 244–5.

cut the already fragile tie that makes a 'populace', of which the urban proletariat is the established metonym, into a unified 'people', which is in turn the basis of state power. The enemy people are bombed so as to destroy their unity and release the underlying forces of anarchy and revolt. In Europe, the people are essentially conceived in relation to the state, the form of their political organization. To bomb the people means destroying the state, or, more precisely, to cause the people to rise against the state. Assuming the lack of coincidence between people and state, the air offensive seeks to undo the unity of the political body and to reduce it to the state of a 'populace'. We must then conclude that national war in the strict sense has never really existed: from its invention, in the revolutionary wars of the late eighteenth century, war between nations dissimulates a class war. The uncertainty as to the nature of the 'people' to bomb – collective sovereign or populace – precisely corresponds to this hidden war that racks nations from within.

Military strategists and political leaders are well aware of this. It is no accident that the totalization of war that took place in the first half of the twentieth century went together with a series of measures aiming to ensure the political and moral cohesion of the population. On the offensive side, the unity of people and state had to be undone, while on the defensive side, the point was to actively construct the unity of a people who would be capable in time of war to resist the famine caused by blockade or air bombing. In practice, this meant taking a whole series of measures of both a social and a material order. Why was the working population so dangerous, particularly in case of war? Quite simply because, as explained in the *Communist Manifesto*, the proletarians had nothing to lose but their chains. Consequently, so as to make them less dangerous, they had to be brought to have something to lose. In short, the experience of the world wars and the perspective of an air war made it necessary not only to build air-raid shelters, but also to develop a social policy that would favour the integration of the working class. The national state, as it was constituted in the nineteenth century, steadily developed into a 'national *social* state'.[32] The state accordingly became capable of actively taking responsibility for class conflict and absorbing it.

The leaders of the workers' movement in the various European countries grasped the possibility opened up by war in 1914 to obtain, in exchange for a truce in the class struggle, a more or less substantial place within the oligarchies in power. This did not mean that social conflict disappeared, rather that it was shifted from a binary opposition into more fragmented forms. The British prime minister Lloyd George devotes some very instructive pages to the conflict between the 'cooperative' leaders and the more radical 'rank and file'.[33] European history in the second half of the twentieth century would experience a series of conflicts between the institutionalized workers' movement on the one hand, and 'autonomy' on the other.[34] If these *'unions sacrées'* were not viewed unanimously by the working population, they undoubtedly had the effect of considerably increasing the influence of the state over civil society. Even in Great Britain, not to speak of the more statized 'Hobbesian' nations on the European continent,

---

32   I have taken the notion of 'social-national state' from Étienne Balibar (see *Droit de cité. Culture et politique en démocratie*, Paris: Éditions de l'aube, 1998, 106).

33   Lloyd George, *War Memoirs*, vol. 4, chapter 'Labour Unrest', particularly 1926, 1937, and 1947.

34   The most obvious example is certainly that of Italy in the 1960s and 1970s. See on this subject Nanni Balestrini and Primo Moroni, *L'Orda d'oro 1968–1977, La grande ondata rivoluzionaria e creativa, politica ed esistenziale*, Milan: Feltrinelli, 2003.

the state became the principal actor in both economic and 'social' fields, the latter now redefined in terms of 'welfare' and managed under state aegis.[35]

To stay with the British example, 'war socialism' implied, for the Liberal Lloyd George, that

> the means of production and distribution were left in private hands so long as the owners conformed to the demands and orders of the State. The system was neither Stalin nor Roosevelt. It fell short of the former's ideas, but went beyond those of the latter.[36]

In short, the war was 'national' only inasmuch as the warring nations managed to contain the underlying social conflict, so that the 'social problem' was absorbed into the national one. With this object, the role of the state had to be strengthened, with more direct intervention into social matters. A national social state had to be created in order to create this nationalized 'people', ready not only to endure famine and bombs, but also to fight against other peoples, similarly nationalized.

National war, of which bombing was the most complete expression, was inseparably bound up with the creation of a new 'people'. The 'populace' was now integrated into a statized community that was at the same time national, social, and 'democratic'. In other words, the national, the social, and the democratic are the necessary flipside of the European wars of the twentieth century: bombing is the hell of a world whose paradise is social security.

---

35 Keith Laybourn, 'Social Welfare: Public and Private, 1900–1930', in Chris Wrigley (ed.), *A Companion to Early Twentieth-Century Britain*, London: Blackwell, 2003, 373–87.

36 Lloyd George, *War Memoirs*, vol. 4, 1930.

CHAPTER 7

Philosophy of the Bomb

The train was crossing the Veneto plain. It began to get very warm in the compartment, to the point that even the distinguished man in his sixties removed his overcoat. Intrigued by this figure, Della Vedova observed him with discreet curiosity. A few minutes before reaching Treviso, the unknown man stood up, carefully folded his coat and placed it on the seat before setting off for the toilet. He hastily returned as the train entered the station, took his case from the luggage net, and picked up his coat, which the train's sharp braking had caused to slip to the ground. He left the train precipitately, though not without acknowledging his travelling companion with a nod of the head. The train set off again, and Della Vedova, now alone in the compartment, noticed on the floor a large yellow envelope that must have fallen from his travelling companion's coat pocket. Impelled by curiosity, the businessman opened it. It contained a large bundle of papers. When he read the title, typed on the first page, his heart began to palpitate: 'Examination of the situation resulting from the occupation of Gorizia, in view of a future declaration of war on Germany'. He feverishly skimmed the text and came across hand-drawn maps indicating the positions of Austrian and Italian troops in the Trento sector. There could be no doubt, this was a military memorandum probably containing confidential information. Was the unknown man on the train a spy? Della Vedova already saw himself being accused of treason and hauled before the courts. So he immediately made for the army headquarters to hand in the embarrassing envelope.

The military authorities launched an investigation to determine where these unsigned papers had come from, and who had left them in the train. Apart from information on military positions at the front, the memorandum contained a bitter criticism of the strategy pursued by the high command, all but accusing General Cadorna of military incompetence. Whereas the recent taking of the town of Gorizia had been hailed as a great victory for the Italian army, this actually had led to a critical situation:

> Without reserves, aware of a scarcity of munitions, all our forces are engaged in an offensive that has already halted, and we are threatened by enemies old and new in the rear. [We may] be attacked at any moment and defeated in a very short space of time.

It goes without saying that the high command had little patience for this kind of criticism in the midst of war. All means were therefore deployed to establish who could have uttered such incendiary statements. The military bureaucracy went into action and an investigation conducted in Rome came upon a promising lead: the elderly man on the train was no other than Gaetano Mosca, professor of constitutional law at the University of Turin, an eminent political scientist, the theorist of political elites, who had recently been appointed under-secretary of state for the colonies. When questioned, he admitted who had given him these papers. It was Colonel Giulio Douhet.

Douhet was not unknown to the hierarchy. A brilliant mind, a writer and journalist in his spare time, he was perceived above all as arrogant and quarrelsome. Early in 1915 (Italy did not declare war on Austria until 23 May of that year) he was sidelined by being posted to Edolo in the Alps. Out of boredom and frustration at having no influence on operations under way, he bombarded his superiors with increasingly critical reports of the high command, calling for a complete change of strategy. Unsurprisingly, these papers disappeared into administrative filing cabinets. An opportunity to short circuit the hierarchy was presented when Gaetono Mosca visited his son who was mobilized on the north-eastern front. The under-secretary took advantage of this trip to meet a number of officers, including General Gortani, who introduced Mosca to his subordinate Douhet. The two men had a number of conversations, and Mosca left with the yellow envelope in his pocket containing Douhet's most recent memorandum, having promised to circulate it among influential circles in Rome.

On 16 September 1916, Colonel Douhet was arrested, stripped of his functions, and brought before a military tribunal. He was accused of having violated at least half a dozen articles of regulations and orders, including one, dated 29 July 1915, that prohibited the expression of any point of view on the war effort that was contrary to information published by the high command. His culpability on this point could not be reasonably put in doubt. Douhet defended himself by appeal to a higher law:

> I conclude by stating vehemently that my mind feels perfectly tranquil because I have done nothing other than obey the supreme law that is etched in the hearts of all of us; that is a law which imposes upon us not to hesitate when we feel the duty falling on us to achieve a common good ... certain that no written law can contradict a supreme natural law; I say surely that no man of heart or conscience can censure a son who utters a cry in order to save the mother of the family.[1]

---

1 Giulio Douhet, 'Auto-difesa,' *L'Eloquenza*, 31 August 1919, Castillo, vols 5–6, 31, quoted by Frank Joseph Cappelluti, *The Life*

On 15 October 1916 the court martial delivered its verdict: guilty. It condemned Colonel Douhet to a year's imprisonment in the fortress of Fenestrelle, and a fine of 170 lire. This humiliation brought an end to what would certainly have been a brilliant military career.

In fact, Douhet's career was far from over, though it took a new direction. His release, in October 1917, coincided with the battle of Caporetto, the greatest military debacle that Italy suffered during the Great War. After the war, a committee charged with investigating the rout concluded that if certain recommendations of the incriminating memorandum of 1916 had been followed, the disaster could have been avoided. Douhet took the opportunity to have his case re-opened, and in November 1920 he was pardoned and promoted to the rank of major-general. After leaving the army, he devoted himself to writing and journalism. Politically close to fascism, he took part in the 'march on Rome' in 1922 and sought to establish a 'fascist air force'.[2] His attempts to resume active service, however, failed in the face of resistance from the military hierarchy.

Posterity will remember Douhet above all as the most accomplished theorist of strategic bombing. His major work, *Command of the Air*, first appeared in 1921, with a second and much-expanded edition in 1926, and still holds a key place in military debate. Its strength lies primarily in its systematic justification of the superiority of the air arm over land and sea forces: for Douhet, only aviation can win a war. The emphasis should be on heavy bombers, used from the start of hostilities against the enemy's infrastructure, industry, and cities. Equipped with explosive

---

and Thought of Giulio Douhet, thesis in modern history at Rutgers University, 1967, 135.

2 Guido Mattiolo, *L'aviazione squadrista. Conferenza tenuta al Guppo Giordani di Roma*, Rome: L'aviazione, 1939, 24–5.

and incendiary bombs, as well as toxic gas, aircraft could rapidly paralyse the adversary, thus bringing the war to a speedy end. The conflict would be unprecedentedly violent, but limited in time; it would certainly cause some tens of thousands of civilian deaths, but – on condition that such outdated notions as the distinction between combatants and non-combatants were abandoned – it would spare millions of soldiers. Douhet's commentators have seen this argument for a merciless attack on civilians as a natural emanation from his commitment to fascism.[3] Does not the strategy of targeting civilians fit perfectly with fascism's characteristic contempt for the human race?

Tempting as this interpretation may be, it comes up against a serious problem. Douhet was not always a champion of bombing. On the contrary: his military reflections belong to a cosmopolitical, even peace-making tradition, and it was initially within this intellectual framework that he built his theoretical construction.

In Douhet's first writings on aviation, published in 1910, he declared categorically,

> No bombardment has ever proved decisive, except when directed at cowards ... Dropping bombs on a city from an airship would be a useless and barbaric act ... The conscience of a man of my century tells me that there are methods it is impossible to use honestly, even in the event of war ... We should not even envisage launching an action against defenceless cities. This would be an act of such barbarism as to revolt the conscience of the civilized world, and would cause more harm to its authors than to its victims.[4]

---

3 See in particular Azar Gatt, *A History of Military Thought from the Enlightenment to the Cold War*, Oxford: Oxford University Press, 2001, chapter 'The Sources of Douhetism', 561–97.

4 Giulio Douhet, 'Le possibilità dell'aeronavigazione', *Rivista*

In lectures given in 1914–15 at the Università Popolare in Turin, then published under the title *The Art of War*, Douhet likewise ruled out any use of the air arm against cities.[5] Yet on 3 July of the same year, Douhet pronounced in favour of the construction of bomber planes. In an article that referred to the ideas of H. G. Wells, he recalled that a German aeroplane had recently made an incursion into French airspace. A few months later, on 20 November, he openly called for the strategic bombing of urban centres.[6] How and why did he radically change his position on this subject in the course of a few months? As we shall see, this strategic choice was intimately bound up, not with his fascist opinions, but with the antinomies of liberal pacifism. However, before exploring this track, it is necessary to say a few words on a man who is, after Machiavelli, the most well-known of Italian strategists.[7]

Giulio Douhet was born on 30 May 1869 in Caserta, a town to the south of Naples, in a military family origi-

---

militare italiana, 7 (1910), 1303–9; republished in G. Douhet, *Scritti 1901–1915*, Rome: Stato Maggiore Aeronautica, Ufficio Storico, 1993, 102.

5   Giulio Douhet, *L'Arte della Guerra, Raccolte di sei conferenze tenute all'Università Popolare Torino 1914–15*, Turin: S. Lattes, 1915, 133–4.

6   'Impressioni e vedute del colonnello cav. Giulio Douhet sull'aviazione militare italiana', published as an appendix in Antonio Pelliccia, *Nessuno è profeta in patria: Riflessioni sulla dottrina del Dominio dell'Aria*, Genoa: SIAG, 1981, 105–13.

7   The following biographical sketch draws above all on the following texts: Cappelluti, *The Life and Thought*; Antonio Monti's introduction to Giulio Douhet, *Scritti inediti*, Florence: Scuola di Guerra Aerea, 1951; Luciano Bozzo, 'Giulio Douhet e il Dominio dell'Aria: Dottrina del "potera aereo" o teoria della Guerra totale?', in Giulio Douhet, *Il dominio dell'aria e altri scritti*, Rome: Aeronautica Militare, Ufficio Storico, 2002, xii–lxiii, and Giorgio Rochate, entry 'Douhet' in *Dizionario biograpfico degli italiani*, Rome: Istituto della Enciclopedia Italiana, 1992, vol. 41, 561–6.

nating from Nice, who had served the house of Savoy for several generations. They settled in Turin when Italy ceded Nice to France. The young Giulio followed the family tradition and enrolled at the School of Artillery. Graduating first of his year, he pursued his studies of military engineering at the Turin Polytechnic School, then at the School of War. After various short-term employments, he was promoted to the rank of captain at the age of thirty-one, and posted to the general staff.

In a series of lectures, Douhet dealt with the mechanization of armed forces, combining technological, tactical, and logistic considerations, though he did not speak of tanks as other military thinkers of the time had begun to do.[8] This lack of reflection on armoured vehicles, and thus on the possibility of conceiving movement on the battlefield after the Great War, would be a constant in his military thought.[9] Another would be his faith in the idea that technological and scientific innovation is the condition for economic growth and military power, particularly for a country such as Italy, the smallest of the European great powers.[10] In 1905, Douhet was appointed to command a unit of *bersaglieri*, an elite motorized force.

From 1904 Douhet won renown as a journalist, signing himself 'Capitano x' in a series of articles on the Russian–Japanese war published in the Genoa daily *Caffaro*. In 1910, he wrote a series of articles on aviation in the

8 Mario Morasso, *La nuova Guerra: armi – combattenti – battaglie*, Milan: Treves, 1914, 163–84.

9 J. F. C. Fuller, *Tanks in the Great War, 1914–1918*, London: John Murray, 1920, 311, and by the same author, *The Conduct of War: A Study on the Impact of the French, Industrial, and Russian Revolutions on War and its Conduct*, London: Methuen, 1972, chapter 'Rebirth of Mobility' (172–7). This book contains a fierce criticism of Douhet's strategic thought (240–2).

10 Giulio Douhet, *Automobilismo militare e pesante*, Genoa: Carlini, 1904, 18; see also Cappelluti, *The Life and Thought*, 10.

specialized press, as well as a series of military memoranda, and two years later was appointed commander of the Italian army's 'aviation battalion'. Against the majority position within the armed forces, which championed dirigibles rather than aeroplanes,[11] he asked his friend, the engineer Giovanni Battista ('Gianni') Caproni to develop heavy bombers, despite having no authorization for this.[12] As a result, Douhet was dismissed from the aviation battalion and posted to the Edolo garrison in the Alps.[13]

Resuming his journalistic activity, Douhet commented on the first eight months of the Great War in a series of 156 articles published under the pseudonym 'Spectator' and published in the Genoa daily *La gazzetta del popolo*.[14] Banned from publication in March 1915, he commenced a *Critical Diary of the War*, later published in two volumes in 1921–22.[15] Convinced that the high command was committing irreparable mistakes, he frenetically drafted memoranda such as the one that Gaetano Mosca left in the train.[16] In his retirement, he worked as a writer and

---

11   See Giuseppe Pesce, *Maurizio Mario Moris: padre dell'-aeronautica italiana*, Gaeta: Stabilimento grafico militare, 1994.

12   See Andrea Curami, 'La nascità dell'industrial aeronautica', in Paolo Ferrari (ed.), *L'aeronautica italiana: una storia del Novecento*, Milan: Franco Angeli, 2004, 13–42, as well as Ferruccio Botti and Mario Cermelli, *La theoria della Guerra aerea in Italia dalle origini alla seconda Guerra mondiale (1884–1939)*, Rome: Stato Maggiore Aeronautica Ufficio Storico, 1989, 180.

13   Gregory Alegi, 'Icaro, Dedalo e i primordi dell'Aeronautica Militare', I Luciano Bozzo (ed.), *Dal futurism al minimalismo: aeronautica e 'potere aereo' nella political internazionale tra XX e XXI secolo*, Naples: Edizioni Scientifiche Italiani, 1999, 45–58.

14   See Giulio Douhet, 'La difesa nazionale', in *La Guerra integrale*, Rome: Campitelli, 1936, 23.

15   Giulio Douhet, *Diario critica de guerra*, Turin: Paravia, 1921 and 1922.

16   Giulio Douhet, *Documenti a complement della rellazione d'inchiesta per Caporetto*, Rome: Dovere, 1919, 5–6.

journalist, dividing his time between Rome and his country house at Porto Potenza Picena on the Adriatic coast. Apart from his military works, he is said to have written several plays and two film scripts, never produced, but none of these works has come down to us. In an ironic destiny for a theorist of bombing, his papers were probably burned in an attack that destroyed the Risorgimento Museum in Milan during the Second World War.

From 1910 onward, Douhet stood out as one of the few Italian specialists on questions of aviation. He was initially sceptical as to the military possibilities this offered: in his view, aeroplanes were fit only for reconnaissance missions.[17] As for bombing, he ruled this out on principle.[18] He did, however, call for an international convention that would prohibit the militarization of the skies before this began.[19] Alongside this position, Douhet presented in the same series of articles his major concept, 'command of the air', which would later provide the title for his best-known book.

Since aviation was undergoing a tremendous technical advance, all armies invested in this new arm, though as yet without having developed any doctrine about its deployment. Douhet's theoretical operation was to apply to the domain of the air Alfred Thayer Mahan's theory of 'command of the seas': the primary objective of air forces was to control the skies, just as that of the navy was to control the waters. The point in both cases was to prevent the adversary from navigating. In case of war, the navy was

17 Giulio Douhet, 'Le possibilità dell'aeronavigazione', *Rivista militare italiana*, 7 (1910), 1303–19, republished in Douhet, *Scritti 1901–1915*, 95–104, in particular 95–6.

18 Ibid., 102.

19 Giulio Douhet, 'La limitazione degli armament navali e la costituzione delle flotte aeree', *Il giornale d'Italia*, (20 August 1910), republished in Douhet, *Scritti 1901–1915*, 106.

to defeat the enemy navy, and the air force to triumph over hostile aviation, so as to obtain 'command' of the milieu. Douhet accordingly estimated that aerial warfare would take place *in* the air, rather than being waged *from* the air.

By taking this position, Douhet opposed those military theorists who envisaged a strategic rather than a tactical use of aviation, and who accordingly relied more on airships than on aircraft.[20] They saw the objective as conducting rapid and violent incursions, in other words, surprise attacks. It was useless to fight in the air with a view to obtaining control of the skies, as this only gave the capacity to attack targets on the ground.[21] The first champions of strategic bombing also drew on naval strategy, yet, unlike Douhet, they did not follow Mahan but rather the French 'Jeune École' and its theory of coastal bombing.

These seemingly very abstract discussions were in no way redundant. On the contrary, they determined orientations of doctrine, and therefore technical ones. For example, an air force that had followed Douhet's precepts in 1910 would have built rather small fighter planes that were easy to manoeuvre, whereas one that banked on bombing would invest in heavy bombers, sacrificing manoeuvrability to payload. In other words, an air force organized according to Douhet's 1910 prescriptions would be technically incapable of burning whole cities.

How was it that this peace-keeping strategy led to the most developed theory of air attack on civilian populations? To understand how these strategic precepts could turn

---

20 According to Henri Mordacq, future head of Clemenceau's private office and later minister of war, airships were suitable for strategic use and aircraft for tactical use. See Henri Mordacq, *La Stratégie, historique, évolution*, Paris: Fournier, 1912, 193.

21 C. M. (Carlo Montù), 'Guerra in aria o dell'aria?', *La Preparazione*, 4–5 August 1910; see also Botti and Cermelli, *La teoria della guerra aerea in Italia*, 56.

into their opposite, we need to examine more closely their conceptual suppositions – since this strategy did implicitly contain a whole political philosophy. Conceptual reversals, moreover, are produced all the more readily when such a philosophy is not spelled out. The idea that war had become 'national' was a constant in Douhet's thought: it was no longer the caprices of princes that pushed nations to war, but rather economic necessities. As a result, the main actors in war were no longer just armies, but rather those complex organizations that are nations.[22]

> Behind every combatant army there is a whole people, rich with all the virtues of its race, and steadily focusing all its energy on the front line, conscious of being engaged in a struggle to the death, where no quarter is given, a combat for existence ... The game is played between nations, and a nation is not defeated until it acknowledges this ... An army can be defeated, a capital can be taken, but a people cannot be destroyed as long as it preserves faith and hope.[23]

If war was national, it was then necessary to defeat the morale of the enemy nation in order to triumph.[24] In the end, the strength of an army is nothing other than the strength of the nation as a whole.[25]

This strength depended on two factors: industrial power

---

22   Giulio Douhet, 'Cause, obbiettivi e modalità del conflitto russo giapponese', *Caffaro*, 14–15 February 1904, reprinted in Douhet, *Scritti 1901–1915*, 37–8; 'Esteti?', *Caffaro*, 2–3 June 1905, in ibid., 76; and *L'Arte della guerra*, 1.

23   Giulio Douhet, 'La grande guerra', *La gazzetta del popolo*, 7 August 1914, in Douhet, *Scritti 1901–1915*, 325–6.

24   Giulio Douhet, 'Chi vincerà?', *La gazzetta del popolo*, 11 August 1914, in ibid., 327.

25   Giulio Douhet, 'La forza della nazione', *La gazzetta del popolo*, 24 February 1915, in ibid., 477–8.

on the one hand, and political, social, and 'moral' cohesion on the other. This combination of an economic element and a political and 'moral' one is clearly very problematic, directly bearing on fundamental questions of liberalism. Douhet's use of the concept of 'nation', in fact, has affinities in some respects with that made by such thinkers as Adam Smith or Emmanuel Sièyes: in each case, the economic is bound up with an underlying political cohesion. In other words, this concept of nation is less 'nationalist', in the modern sense of the term, than political: it denotes either the community of citizens and their attachment to the *res publica* – a definition of the nation that is certainly not far removed from a democratic one[26] – or else something like 'civil society', a concept that likewise links economic determinations with a 'public opinion'.[27] At all events, the concept of nation that Douhet deployed was not 'totalitarian', inasmuch as it emphasized the spontaneous adhesion of citizens to the community and its values.[28]

On the other hand, government action and political stability also play a far from negligible role in his political reflections: the 'people' are not simply the foundation of all political cohesion, they are also a factor of destabilization. Political power thus needs to contain this 'people' in order

26 See Eric Hobsbawm, *Nations and Nationalism since 1780: Programme, Myth, Reality*, Ithaca: Cornell University Press, 2009. It is true, however, that in certain places Douhet himself follows a more 'nationalist' or even racial definition of the nation: 'Lotta di razze', *La gazzetta del popolo*, 26 August 1914, in *Scritti 1901–1915*, 337–8.

27 Giulio Douhet, 'La vana minaccia', *La gazzetta del popolo*, 25 February 1915, in ibid., 479.

28 Several formulations run in this sense. We need only cite Giulio Douhet, 'Il compenso', *Caffaro*, 15–16 January 1905, in ibid., 67–9; 'Disciplina', *La gazzetta del popolo*, 19 September 1914, in ibid., 368–71; 'Il perché', 18 October 1914, in ibid., 390–3; as well as 'Le energie del popolo per la resistenza', in *Scritti inediti*, pp. 72–81, especially 73.

to impose order. From this point of view, the concept of 'nation' that sits at the heart of Douhet's reflections on war is broadly in line with republican thought, and even modern democratic thought. As a source of both political unity and destabilization, the nation is not only the principal actor in modern war, it is simultaneously its target.[29] If it is 'faith and hope' that decide the outcome of a war, then it is these moral dispositions that must be attacked in the enemy nation.

The 'nation' also possesses a further determination, distinct from the sense acquired by the concept since the late nineteenth century: it is no longer defined in opposition to other nations, and 'nationalism' in no way rules out a cosmopolitan dimension. Douhet thus reactivated an older political semantics, according to which, to quote Eric Hobsbawm, nations are simply 'a second-best to world unity'.[30] In this perspective, Douhet borrowed from the tradition bequeathed by the Enlightenment the idea of a 'European civil society' linked to a transnational public opinion, and explained that 'civilized nations produce public opinion, which sees with its own eyes and judges as a function of its own mentality; they constitute a kind of public that judges by basing itself more on sentiment than on cold logic'.[31]

The nation is based on 'society', and both concepts are transnational by nature. Public opinion, itself also transnational, decides what is just or unjust, in the manner of a tribunal of practical reason. It is not surprising that, in the context of the First World War, this 'international public opinion' that represents society and civilization should

---

29 Giulio Douhet, 'La grande guerra', 326.
30 Hobsbawm, *Nations and Nationalism*, 31.
31 Giulio Douhet, 'La cultura', *La gazzetta del popolo*, 6 October 1914, in *Scritti 1901–1915*, 383–5.

have been equated with the public opinion of the countries united in the Entente – in other words, the army to which Douhet himself belonged. The enemy, embodied by the Central Powers, was guilty of 'militarism': its

> policy of force is not always the best; for a nation as for an individual, it is not enough to make oneself feared, it is also necessary to be loved. Man does not just have his fists, he also has a heart and a spirit ... Violent and unjust action provokes a reaction all the more violent in that it is just.[32]

Not only did Douhet universalize the public opinion of one warring party by conferring on it the right to decide on the justice or injustice of warlike actions; the justice of its struggle authorized it to employ still more violent means. The argument may seem perfectly logical: violence is inherently reprehensible, it can only be justified by a just cause; ergo, only one party engaged in a conflict can stand in a position of justice. As a result, there is every chance that the question is settled empirically; the struggle of the winner will have been just, and that of the defeated unjust. It was precisely for that reason that classical international law had excluded this question, conferring on each state an equal right to war: since a struggle for 'justice' involved every risk of a totalization of war, it was better to fight for political objectives, which were necessarily limited.

But that is not all. Astonishing as it may seem for a career army officer, Douhet asserted that war was contrary to nature:

---

32 Giulio Douhet, 'La più barbara guerra?', *La gazzetta del popolo*, 20 August 1914, in ibid., 331–3.

War represents an abnormal situation for human society. True, the fact that humanity may be subject to this type of abnormal crisis at almost regular intervals shows that a long road has still to be run in order for him to develop, that human society is far from being perfect and that men of good will must cooperate in a sacred duty: that of improving the humanity to which they belong; of perfecting human society, freeing it from this lasting nightmare that maintains it in a terrible subjection, this kind of collective epilepsy that transfigures and distorts the face of humanity.[33]

These lines, published in 1915, seem closer to pacifism than to fascism. War was an abnormal state, contrary to what defined humanity, which was to live peacefully in society. War exists because the history of humanity has not yet reached its end, the peaceful union of all peoples. This 'human nature' for which Douhet burned to fight during the First World War is progressively realized in a teleological history. Two moral imperatives follow from this: it is necessary to hasten the march of history and combat those who wish to set back a humanity engaged on the path of justice and peace. As for the end of this history, Douhet conceptualized this with what international relations theorists call the 'domestic analogy', in other words, by conceiving a supranational power on the model of state power:[34] 'to this day, there is still no law or sanction governing nations, and for nations, force remains the ultimate means of settling disputes'.[35]

Human beings have established a national 'society' protected by the coercive means of the state, and thus created

---

33 Douhet, *L'Arte della guerra*, 4–5.
34 See Chiara Bottici, *Men and States: Rethinking the Domestic Analogy in a Global Era*, Basingstoke: Palgrave Macmillan, 2009.
35 Douhet, *L'Arte della guerra*, 4–5.

a sentiment of fraternity and community; but since on the international level these ties are lacking or insufficiently developed, peoples are opposed to one another. Humanity thus has the sacred duty of working for its perfection, meaning the perfecting of a transnational 'society'. How can this come about? Douhet's response, quite unambiguous, was directly inspired by a peace-making tradition according to which peace can only be established and maintained if there exists a supranational power capable of containing the authors of disturbance on the international level:

> An agreement among all nations, in order to impose on all respect for treaties and international law, would introduce into relations between nations the principle on which justice rests in relations between individuals: no one has the right to render justice themselves ... It is consequently necessary to introduce into the international context the sanctions and means of applying them that already exist within national borders.[36]

The word 'justice' reappears – not in a substantial sense, but in the sense of jurisdiction: no nation has the right to render justice to itself, 'justice' can only emanate from an international body. Douhet thus pleaded for the establishment of an 'international tribunal' founded on a world 'Magna Carta':

> All nations must agree on respect for the Magna Carta and the verdicts delivered by the international Tribunal; which would naturally presuppose the establishment of a kind of international gendarmerie capable of having such

---

36 Giulio Douhet, 'Incursione in Utopia', *La gazzetta del popolo*, 5 March 1915, reprinted in *Scritti 1901–1915*, 491–3.

measures respected. This international gendarmerie would replace the present armies and navies ... The international Tribunal would be made up of the most illustrious men of all nations, and each nation would have a vote equal to the number of its inhabitants, since all men in the world are equal; and the verdicts of this supreme Tribunal would be applied if need be by military means ... The coexistence of nations would lose the status of an anarchic relationship to become civil cohabitation. It would mean an end to abuses of power, authoritarian actions, the brutal use of force designed to suspend all law; it would mean an end to war, at most there would occasionally be clashes between gendarmes and malefactors.[37]

The establishment of an international power capable of imposing these decisions, by force if need be, would make it possible to abolish war, as a relationship between states, in favour of international 'police' operations. The prevailing anarchy at the level of international relations would be replaced by a world republic of civilization. It goes without saying that this also implies a radical transformation in the image of the enemy. During the period running by and large from the end of the Thirty Years War to the First World War, the enemy – at least in Europe – was honoured as 'just' if he constituted a legitimate power (legitimacy *ad bellum*) and respected the fundamental rules of war (*in bello*). In the course of the First World War, warfare became asymmetrical: soon it would no longer oppose two equally respectable adversaries, but become a police action directed against malefactors. It is quite remarkable how this 'asymmetrical' character of war, of which much is written today, was initially related to a moral asymmetry, before being translated onto the levels of weapons and

---

37   Ibid., 492.

tactics. A moral asymmetry inscribed in a teleological philosophy of history.

Justice was one of the concepts that Douhet borrowed from the European Enlightenment tradition. The attribute of justice traditionally served to distinguish legitimate power, which should be obeyed, from usurped power, which should be resisted. Justice was an integral aspect of peace, inasmuch as it enabled true peace to be distinguished from mere oppression. For St Augustine, for example, peace was 'the tranquillity of order', and order – corresponding to the definition of justice given in the Platonic tradition – the 'disposition of beings according to their place'.[38] Conceived initially as a divine emanation, justice would become in the age of Enlightenment an eminently human characteristic. There is justice in a 'human' institutional and political framework, one capable of evolving in the course of a history oriented towards the realization of humanity. It was precisely in these terms that Douhet conceptualized war and peace: peace, justice, and humanity stood at the end of the historical process. Correlatively, war, injustice, and inhumanity were survivors from a barbaric age.

Every argument founded on the notion of 'humanity', however, precisely risks dehumanizing the enemy. If justice is an attribute of humanity, injustice logically pertains to inhumanity. The American philosopher William Ernest Hocking thus explained in 1918 that, since army and nation were now simply one, populations are impregnated with a 'fighting spirit':

> What makes humanity is the power of the human being to commit himself to an idea or principle and to stand for it,

38 'Pax omnium rerum tranquillitas ordinis. Ordo est parium dispariumque rerum sua cuique loca tribuens disposition.' St Augustine, *The City of God*, Book 19, Chapter 11.

so that the conflict of the principles becomes a conflict of the men who stand for them. My enemy is the man who is standing for what I am bound to regard as a bad principle ... to keep that false idea from getting a hold in the world, to exclude that bad principle, means on account of his choice, to exclude *him* ... The object of warfare is not to exclude individual souls from the universe: it is to keep their false choices from polluting the stream of history from which our descendants – and theirs – must draw their life.[39]

The tone is clearly set: the object of war is to exclude the bearers of evil principles, so as to prevent the universe and history from being infected. For Douhet, the 'evil principle' to be extirpated is named 'militarism':

The man who takes up arms to violate the rights of another commits a criminal act: just as criminal is the nation that takes up arms to impose its will on the nations among whom it lives. Militarism, conceived in this way, is something barbarous and uncivilized; it is repugnant to the developed man and revolts the sentiments of equilibrium and justice ... Against this militarism, synonymous with international banditry, both the world and the population of the country that created it must rise up: no one should be complicit with a criminal act.[40]

Every person is summoned to combat 'evil principles', even if these are conveyed by the government of their own nation. Here again, the analysis is set in a 'democratic' framework: citizens are responsible for the action of their

---

39 William Ernest Hocking, *Morale and Its Enemies*, New Haven: Yale University Press, 1918, 60.

40 Giulio Douhet, 'Militarismo', *La gazzetta del popolo*, 9 September 1914, reprinted in *Scritti 1901–1915*, 557–9.

governments, both collectively and individually. We should thus guard against explaining the strategic options that Douhet would champion some years later in terms of 'fascism': on the contrary, the deliberate attack on civilian populations was a possibility inherent to modern 'democratic' political integration, in the same way that fascism was one historical possibility among others of institutionalizing popular sovereignty.[41]

Douhet drew from this argument a conclusion that was scarcely surprising. Aerial bombing, as an absolute weapon capable of absolute destruction, could only be legitimately employed with an absolute aim in mind: humanity. It was thus completely logical that the strategist proposed the placing of the new weapon under the control of a cosmopolitan power, as a means by which this power would ensure the execution of its decisions.[42] Quite evidently, this intellectual construction comes up against a concrete problem: there is no supranational power representing international justice. In practice, therefore, universalist justice must be the responsibility of particular nations. From this point of view, the doctrines of air warfare developed in the inter-war years were a logical extension of those of the First World War: the different 'war aims' were no longer dictated simply by the realpolitik of particular states, but represented an aspiration to universalism. On the side of the Western powers, the slogan of 'civilization' was replaced by that of 'democracy', while on the side of the German contender, expansionist culturalism was radicalized in the form of Nazism. With the Soviet Union, a

---

41 Giorgio Agamben proposes 'the thesis of a deep solidarity between democracy and totalitarianism', *Homo sacer*, Stanford: Stanford University Press, 1988, 10.

42 Giulio Douhet, 'Sottomarini ed aeroplani', in *Scritti inediti*, 154–72, especially 170–1.

new contender appeared on the horizon, representing another form of universalism, that of an international class struggle controlled by the bureaucratic elite in the Kremlin.

If Douhet became the most important theorist of air warfare, and his works retain a key importance, this is above all because *Command of the Air* offered airmen the world over a coherent justification for the capacities of their weapon. In other words, the work aroused the interest it did, especially in the English-speaking world, not by the novelty of its strategic precepts, but by the fact that it presented these in a coherent manner. It is all the more surprising that the political and philosophical foundations of this military argument[43] have been very largely ignored.[44]

Douhetism can be defined by three strategic theses. First of all, aerial supremacy (command of the air) is a primordial factor in war, and no large-scale operation, whether on land or sea, is possible without domination of the sky. Then, aviation is a weapon best employed in an autonomous fashion, in other words as an independent strategic weapon rather than a support for land or naval forces. It follows that air forces must be institutionally independent rather than subordinated to the army or navy. And finally, aviation is an essentially offensive weapon. Clausewitz's proposition according to which defence is more economical than attack does not apply to aviation, since it is extremely complicated to defend the skies against enemy incursions. Aviation is a strike force, a force of pure attack. By its almost unlimited destructive capacity, it can decide by itself the outcome of a war. Once the enemy declares

43   A fuller discussion can be found in Thomas Hippler, *Bombing the People: Giulio Douhet and the Origins of Air Power Strategy*, Cambridge: Cambridge University Press, 2013.

44   Even in Italy, the texts of the 'young Douhet', cosmopolitan and even pacifist, remained unknown until Curami and Rochat published his *Scritti 1901–1915* in 1993.

himself defeated, police forces are sufficient to occupy his territory. As a result, the Douhetists recommended focusing on air power, backed up by chemical weapons and later by nuclear bombs and intercontinental missiles. Douhetism would be a key strategic option in future twentieth-century conflicts, starting with the Second World War.

It is impossible to say how Douhet, who died in 1930, would have analysed this conflict, which saw his country, Italy, allied to the German contender, and not, as in the First World War, on the side of the Western powers struggling for civilization and democracy against militarism. But it was during the Second World War that his ideas would be put into practice on a large scale for the first time: the strategic bombing campaigns against Germany and Japan were simply the realization of his doctrines.

CHAPTER 8

Making and Unmaking a People

Many people had found refuge that evening in a dark and narrow cellar converted into an air-raid shelter. Most of them were unknown to the small community that had already been gathering there for years, every time that the siren sounded the alarm. Ilse Grassmann looked at them, trying to make out who they were and where they came from. The little backpack containing everything necessary for survival said a great deal about the character of its owner, equally the elegant suitcase of the lady wearing a fur coat in this hot month of July. Some individuals, less bourgeois in appearance, had hastily packed up all their possessions. Others again had been forced to abandon their baggage in another cellar or on the pavement, unable to rescue more than their own life and the clothes on their back. In one corner, Ilse Grassmann noticed a woman covered in bandages, her eyes closed. With her hands she mechanically reassured herself of the presence of her two children: was she thinking of the two others she had lost on the road, in smoke and flames?

Suddenly the bombs began to rain down. One explosion followed another nonstop. The building shook, the ground trembling beneath the concrete. Paralysed by fear, the cellar's inhabitants notices pillars shift and cracks appear in the ceiling. Each shell made a deafening noise, followed by a few seconds of anxious silence. One violent impact, very close by, tore the metal door off its hinges, and the cellar was filled with smoke and dust. One more, and the light went out. Panic was noticeable on everyone's face. The

Bunkerwart explained that several buildings in the street had already caught fire. The cellar had to be evacuated as soon as possible, if its occupants were not to be burned alive or buried beneath the debris of the collapsing building. The picture outside was impossible to describe: two buildings at the corner of the street were aflame like gigantic torches against the dark sky. Fire was coming from everywhere, the air was crackling, burning, sizzling. The roof seemed to float in the sky, before the fire descended storey by storey.[1]

'Operation Gomorrah', the intentional firestorm unleashed in July 1943, was the greatest success so far of the bombing offensive. The mission order given on 27 May by Sir Arthur Harris, head of Bomber Command, could not have been more clear: 'aim: destroy Hamburg'. The city centre was turned into a single gigantic fire, the temperature rose to 800 degrees, and a wind of 240 km/h tore through the streets. Some 35,000 people perished in the flames. The number of wounded is estimated at anywhere from 80,000 to 125,000.[2]

The air offensives of the Second World War against Germany and Japan were typical examples of 'Douhetism'.[3]

---

1 Ilse Grassmann, 'Ausgebombt', in Volker Hage, *Hamburg 1943. Literarische Zeugnisse zum Feuersturm*, Hamburg: Fischer, 2003, 217–30 (extract from a diary kept between 1943 and 1945).

2 The fullest documentation of the effects of the air war on Hamburg is found in Hans Brunswig, *Feuersturm über Hamburg: Die Luftangriffe auf Hamburg im Zweiten Weltkrieg und ihre Folgen*, Stuttgart: Motorbuch Verlag, 1978. A number of similar accounts are collected in Klaus Schmidt (ed.), *Die Brandnacht. Dokumente von der Zerstörung Darmstadts am 11. September 1944*, Darmstadt: Reba-Verlag, 1964.

3 Anonymous, 'The Doctrines of General Douhet: A Controversy', *Military Review*, 12/49 (1933), 18–23; Robert A. Pape, *Bombing to Win: Air Power and Coercion in War*, Ithaca: Cornell University Press, 1996, 92.

If the question of Douhet's influence remains debated among historians,[4] it is undeniable that the air strategy practised by Great Britain and the United States followed closely the precepts of the Italian theorist.[5] Allied bombers dropped 1.3 million tons of bombs on Germany, destroying more than 40 per cent of the built-up area of the seventy largest cities and killing approximately 380,000 people.[6] According to the assessment made after the war by the US authorities (the United States Strategic Bombing Survey), strategic bombing had caused half a million fatalities.[7]

---

4   B. Greenhous, 'A Speculation on Giulio Douhet and the English Connection', in *La figura e l'opera di Giulio Douhet*, Caserta: Società di Storia di Terra di Lavoro, 1988, 41–52; R. R. Flugel, *United States Air Power Doctrine: A Study on the Influence of William Mitchell and Giulio Douhet at the Air Corps Tactical School*, PhD thesis, University of Oklahoma, 1965; James S. Corum, *The Luftwaffe: Creating the Operational War, 1918–1940*, Lawrence: University Press of Kansas, 1997, 89–90; Bernard Brodie, *Strategy in the Missile Age*, Princeton: Princeton University Press 1965, 73; J. L. Boone Atkinson, 'Italian Influence on the Origins of the American Concept of Strategic Bombing', *The Air Power Historian*, 4/3 (1957), 141–9. Douhet's influence is challenged for example by R. D. S. Higham, *The Military Intellectuals in Britain, 1918–1939*, New Brunswick: Rutgers University Press, 1966, 257.

5   H. H. Arnold, *Global Mission*, New York: Harper and Brothers, 1949, 131, and S. P. Rosen, *Winning the Next War: Innovation and the Modern Military*, Ithaca: Cornell University Press, 1991, 150.

6   Olaf Groeher, 'Der strategische Luftkrieg und seine Auswirkungen auf die deutsche Zivilbevölkerung', in Horst Boog (ed.), *Luftkriegführung im Zweiten Weltkrieg. Ein internationaler Vergleich*, Herford: E. S. Mittler & Sohn 1993, 329–49, especially 343; United States Strategic Bombing Survey (USSBS), *Summary Report (European War)*, Washington, DC: GPO, 1945, 36, and Kenneth Hewitt, 'Place Annihilation: Area Bombing and the Fate of Urban Places', *Annals of the Association of American Geographers*, 73/2 (1983), 257–84.

7   USSBS No. 65, Medical Branch, *The Effects of Bombing on Health and Medical Care in Germany*, quoted by Dietmar Süss, *Death From the Skies: How the British and Germans Survived Bombing in World War II*, Oxford: Oxford University Press, 2014, 6.

The estimates of the German authorities were 410,000 civilian victims, 32,000 'foreigners and prisoners of war', and 23,000 army and police personnel.[8] And yet, despite this massive destruction, Germany only capitulated after Berlin fell to ground troops – thus making this strategic bombing campaign the most flagrant example of the failure of Douhetism.

The case of Japan was slightly different: on the one hand, because of the perfecting of Douhetism in the form of the atom bomb, and on the other hand, because Japan, contrary to Germany, was one of the very rare cases in which a great power capitulated without a large part of its territory being occupied. We can surely maintain that strategic bombing proved militarily ineffective in Germany: even without the bombing, the war would have ended in the same way and at almost the same time.[9] The question of Japan is more complex, and its capitulation is often ascribed to the effects of the atom bomb. Yet there are good reasons for believing that in this case too, neither conventional nor nuclear bombing was the decisive factor.

In Germany, the Allied forces conceived four different strategies, each of which was firmly based on strategic aviation.[10] The first of these, the 'industrial network' theory, was the air doctrine practised by the United States at the time of its entry into the war. This concentrated on a

---

8 Helmut Schnatz, 'Die Zerstörung der deutschen Städte und die Opfer', in Bernd Heidenreich and Sönke Neitzel (eds), *Der Bombenkrieg und seine Opfer*, Wiesbaden: Hessische Landeszentrale für politische Bildung, 2004, 30–48, and Süss, *Death From the Skies*, 6.

9 This is despite the fact that in certain cases bombing did succeed in destroying social ties. See the interesting article by Neil A. Gregor, '"Schicksalsgemeinschaft"? Allied Bombing, Civilian Morale, and Social Dissolution in Nuremberg, 1942–1945', *Historical Journal*, 43/4 (2000), 1051–70.

10 The following paragraphs draw largely on Pape, *Bombing to Win*, 258–60.

limited number of key sectors: though its priorities varied in the course of the war, it targeted above all the electricity network, the transport network (railways, canals, motor-ways), and the oil infrastructure. According to this theory, the destruction of these vulnerable and circumscribed points would lead to the country's economic collapse, followed by a popular revolt that would in turn bring about the fall of the Nazi government. For this reason, the doctrine envisaged attacking the urban population, and particularly that of the capital, once the destruction of industrial centres had borne its fruit.

The American approach thus saw its mission terminating with what the British air force placed at the start of its operations: 'morale bombing', in other words, deliberate attack on the most densely populated cities with a view to destroying the morale of the civilian population, initially with explosive bombs, then from 1942 with the use of incendiaries. The heads of the RAF set themselves a double objective: 'first, we must make [German towns] physically uninhabitable and, secondly, we must make the people conscious of constant personal danger. The immediate aim is therefore two-fold, namely to produce: (i) destruction; and (ii) the fear of death.'[11] According to an official document, the British aim was to destroy 6 million dwellings, which would create 25 million homeless, kill 900,000 people, and injure a further million, by dropping 1.25 million tons of bombs.

The third strategy, which in 1943 replaced that of the 'industrial network', can be described as 'strategic interdiction'. This focused on those sectors of the enemy system

---

11   Air Staff, 'The Value of Incendiary Weapons in Attack on Area Targets', 29 September 1941, in Towns Panel of the British Bombing Survey Units, *Effects of Strategic Air Attacks on German Towns*, London: HMSO, 1947, 50, quoted by Pape, *Bombing to Win*, 261.

directly linked to the combat strength of the armed forces, whereas the 'industrial network' theory aimed to destroy targets more upstream in the industrial chain. This reorientation became necessary after the unqualified verdict delivered by a committee charged with studying the German economy: the 'industrial network' theory had underestimated the enemy's capacity to replace and repair damaged installations. Electric power stations accordingly disappeared from the top of the list of US targets, replaced by the ball-bearing industry needed by motor vehicles and thus for equipping the German armed forces with vehicles and tanks.

The final strategic option, embarked on in 1943, proceeded from the assumption that an invasion of Germany was unavoidable. The strategy of bombing alone was thus recognized as a failure. Before this date, the Allies, and the British in particular, believed that only the Red Army had the military capacity to defeat the Wehrmacht on the ground: the contribution of the Western powers to the war effort could not be more than the air war. The strategy applied in Europe was thus the same as had been practised for almost a quarter of a century in the colonies with greater or lesser success: to conquer without the awkwardness of occupation. The reasons for abandoning this strategy were many: first of all, the Soviet Union insistently demanded the opening of a second front in Europe; then, the Cold War was already looming on the horizon and the Western powers, particularly the United States, did not want to see the whole of German territory fall into the hands of the USSR. Less than a year before the end of the conflict, at a point when the outcome of the war was almost settled on the eastern front – without strategic bombing – the Allied forces landed in Normandy. An air campaign of 'operational interdiction' supported their advance by attacking the German army's supply chain (armaments, munitions, foodstuffs), as well as railways, ports, and roads in the rear.

As far as Japan was concerned, the chronology was rather different. When the war in the Pacific began, the Americans relied primarily on a naval blockade against a country that was particularly vulnerable in view of its dependence on imported raw materials. This strategy took time to produce its effects, but they were decisive: in July 1945, Japan's productive capacity was reduced almost to nothing.[12] Bombing, on the other hand, was technically difficult on account of the distance of Japan from any US bases. The country only came within range of its aircraft in summer 1944, with the capture of the Mariana Islands. For this reason, the USAF confined itself initially to contributing to an interdiction campaign waged under the aegis of naval forces.

The reorientation of 1945 is partly explained by the rivalry between different services. The US Navy could claim to have annihilated the enemy's economic power, precisely calculating the tonnages it had sunk, whereas the effects of precision bombing were far harder to quantify, a considerable handicap in the battle of numbers that began to rage between the land, sea, and air forces. Despite the resistance of USAF representatives, in July 1944 the Joint War Plans Committee set the invasion of Japan as an objective to attain. The Air Force accordingly saw itself in an awkward position for the budget negotiations that would take place after the war: how could they argue that air power was the decisive weapon if the war ended, both in Asia and in Europe, with a classic invasion of enemy territory? The Air Force had to be able to claim that it had created the conditions for an invasion. Not only to obtain calculable results,

---

12   Pape, *Bombing to Win*, 134–5.

but also images that American cinemas could present in their news programmes; spectacular results that would strike public opinion were the ideal solution.

This is how the most deadly strategic bombing campaign in history was launched. It began only belatedly, on 9 March 1945, with an incendiary raid on Tokyo that claimed between 84,000 and 100,000 fatalities. As the greater part of Japan's housing stock was built of wood, between a quarter and a half of the city's surface area disappeared in the flames. Over the following months, the USAF attacked sixty-six other cities, each time destroying around 40 per cent of their area. Twenty-two million people, or 30 per cent of the Japanese population, were made homeless. The total number of dead (900,000) was greater than that of soldiers killed in combat (780,000). Japan only escaped chemical and biological weapons thanks to Churchill's veto; he feared that the use of such weapons against Japan would provide Germany with a pretext to deploy them against Britain. The atom bomb, on the other hand, was used on 6 and 9 August 1945, well after German capitulation, against a country whose urban centres had already been largely destroyed by conventional firebombs.

Japan capitulated on 15 August 1945, to the great joy of USAF strategists and apologists for the atom bomb: was it not clear that air power and the nuclear weapon had brought the war to an end? This spectacular event, however, hid other factors that were actually decisive: in August 1945, a large part of Japan's industrial capacity had been destroyed, its oil reserves were exhausted, the Japanese army had met with crushing defeat by the Soviet Union in Manchuria, and a US invasion was imminent. In short, Japan would have capitulated in any case, and at almost the same time. The effectiveness of air power, and even of the atom bomb, was largely exaggerated.

As distinct from the bombing of Japan, which lasted only six months, that of Germany lasted five years, but followed a more varying rhythm. Until July 1941, the RAF suspended its doctrine of 'morale bombing' in favour of operational interdiction, firstly because London, far nearer the front line than Berlin, was afraid of reprisals, and also to brake the German advance by attacking first of all their sources of oil supply and the rail stations used by their army, followed by their aircraft industry. Starting in 1942, the RAF returned to its favoured strategy of 'morale bombing', joined by the USAF in 1944. The Americans, for their part, initially counted on strategic interdiction, on several occasions attacking Schweinfurt where half the Axis's ball-bearings production was concentrated. Despite the damage inflicted, however, production was only temporarily interrupted, and the Wehrmacht does not seem to have suffered any resulting shortage. This led to a change of strategy in the period before the opening of a second front on the West. The accent was now shifted to oil installations and transport.[13]

Despite these hesitations, oscillations, and changes of priority, the Allies never renounced attacking the most densely populated areas, even when it became obvious that the war would not end with an internal collapse of the Reich. Trenchard's prediction that the enemy government would sue for peace under pressure of a bombed-out population did not come true. Rather than changing strategy,

---

13   See in particular Walt Whitman Rostow, *Pre-Invasion Bombing Strategy: General Eisenhower's Decision of March 25, 1944*, Austin: University of Texas Press, 1981, also Wesley Frank Craven and James Lea Cate (eds), *Army Air Forces in World War II, Volume 3, Europe: Argument to V-E-Day January 1944 to May 1945*, Chicago: University of Chicago Press, 1951, 67–79, 138–66 and 172–81, and Charles Webster and Noble Frankland, *The Strategic Air Offensive against Germany 1939–1945*, vol. 3, part 5, 10–41.

the Allies resorted to increasingly racist justifications, such as that given by Churchill in April 1941: 'There are less than seventy million malignant Huns – some of whom are curable and others are killable'.[14] However, whether it was a question of pressing the population to revolt, 'curing' them, or killing them, the task of aviation proved harder than envisaged. It became rapidly apparent that attacks with classic explosive bombs generally killed fewer than a thousand people, which was rather disappointing and certainly quite insufficient to obtain the desired result.

It was soon realized that a city is too large to be destroyed by explosives, and that combustion is the only way to a decisive effect. Modern brick-built housing, combined with the presence of firewalls and well-trained fire-fighters, were difficult obstacles to overcome, not to mention the very low precision of air bombing. An official report of 1941, the 'Butt Report', took the measure of this failure. Even if 'success' was defined as any drop in a radius of 8 kilometres around a target, only one bomber in three managed to actually strike its objective. Worse, these figures were for the total of all operations conducted in all theatres of war. If only German home territory was taken into account, the results were still more disappointing: one successful bombing out of four for the country as a whole, one in ten for the industrial region of the Ruhr, and one in fifteen on nights of a new moon.[15]

The champions of 'morale bombing', however, far from admitting defeat, met the conclusions of the Butt Report with a response disarming in its simplicity. If it was

14 Quoted by Stephen A. Garrett, *Ethics and Airpower in World War II: The British Bombing of German Cities*, New York: St. Martin's Press, 1993, 91.

15 Norman Longmate, *The Bombers: The RAF Offensive Against Germany, 1939–1945*, London: Hutchington, 1983, 120–6, especially 121.

GOVERNING FROM THE SKIES

complicated to strike with precision, all that was needed was to choose a sufficiently large target, such as a city with a radius more than 8 kilometres, and attack it with a large enough number of planes. If explosives did not cause enough damage, then incendiaries should be used. An armada of experts was then charged with scientifically studying these problems and proposing technical solutions. Mathematicians calculated the statistical risk of collision in these gigantic air fleets, but the most important contribution was provided by fire engineers, who most often came from established fire brigades.[16]

After the theoretical calculations came practical experimentation. In the state of Utah, 100 kilometres south-west of Salt Lake City, the architect Erich Mendelsohn built a 'German village'. A champion of modernism in the Weimar period, Mendelsohn's ambition was to create a new housing culture. A refugee first of all in Britain, then in the United States, he was charged in 1943 with reconstituting German working-class dwellings as faithfully as possible. Following the advice of an expert from the Harvard department of architecture, timber was brought from Murmansk, which soldiers sprayed with water to obtain a degree of humidity comparable with that in Berlin. Stage designers from the RKO studios, helped by colleagues who had worked in Germany, rebuilt the typical interior of a Berlin working-class family in the smallest details. These buildings were

---

16 James K. McElroy, 'The Work of the Fire Protection Engineers in Planning Fire Attacks', in Horacio Bond (ed.), *Fire and the Air War: A Compilation of Expert Observations on Fires of the War set by Incendiaries and the Atomic Bombs, Wartime Fire Fighting, and the Work of the Fire Protection Engineers who Helped Plan the Destruction of Enemy Cities and Industrial Plants*, Boston National Fire Protection Association, 1946, 122–34. Also Jörg Friedrich, *The Fire: The Bombing of Germany, 1940–1945*, New York: Columbia University Press, 2008.

then reduced to ashes by incendiary bombs, to enable the engineers to study the propagation of fire. Finally, Utah state prisoners rebuilt the village and the cycle began again.[17]

To remedy the poor precision of the bombing raids pointed out by the Butt Report, in 1942 the RAF established a squadron specialized in the localization of targets, made up of experienced pilots. These 'pathfinders' flew at the head of the main fleet, using lighting bombs to mark out the zones to be bombed. The 'master bomber', nicknamed 'master of ceremonies', orbited above the others, guiding his colleagues by radio. In successive waves, the bombers dropped their loads within the perimeter indicated by the flares. The first attack was conducted with explosives. Heavy bombs ripped through buildings from top to bottom, their detonations exploding doors and windows, an essential condition for air flow, and destroying water pipes, thus condemning fire-fighters to impotence. Lighter bombs tore off roofs, exposing beams and attics – the most inflammable parts of buildings, fortunately located on top. Conditions were then met for the second wave of attack with incendiaries, provoking an enormous fire and the combustion of the entire city.

Contrary to the image of omnipotence conveyed by aviation, the mortality rate in bomber squadrons was particularly high. Out of 125,000 men deployed on the planes of Britain's Bomber Command in the course of the Second World War, there were a total of 73,741 losses – dead, wounded, or prisoner. Once recruited by Bomber

---

17 Mike Davis, 'Berlin's Skeleton in Utah's Closet', in *Dead Cities: And Other Tales*, New York: The New Press, 2002; and 'Angriff auf German Village', in Stephan Burgdorff and Christian Habbe (eds), *Als Feuer vom Himmel fiel: Der Bombenkrieg in Deutschland*, Bonn: Bundeszentrale für politische Bildung, 2004, 85–8.

Command it was the custom to carry out thirty missions. With a rate of loss of 3.3 per cent per mission, this statistically represented a minimal chance of survival. In the first attack on Berlin, at the end of August 1943, the RAF lost 7.9 per cent of the airmen engaged; the USAF paid an equally high price for its temporary destruction of German ball-bearing factories on 17 August: a third of the planes sent over Schweinfurt were brought down. In short, not only was the bombing of urban populations at the opposite extreme from the knightly ideal that had been cultivated between the wars, but serving on board a bomber was akin to a suicide mission.

The strategic bombing campaigns of the Second World War still arouse unease today, and it seems hard to separate historical analysis from a normative evaluation. The writer W. G. Sebald maintained in 1999 that German literature had failed to take into account the trauma caused by the bombing.[18] In fact, despite the existence of a number of specialized studies, the air war remained strangely absent from both historiography and collective memory until the publication of Jörg Friedrich's book *The Fire* in 2002, the first to be devoted to the suffering of the German civilian population. Its author had already won acclaim for previous books on the subjects of Nazi justice[19] and the war of extermination waged by the German army in the Soviet Union,[20] so he could scarcely be suspected of revisionist inclinations. Yet his book on the air war provoked a heated discussion, and he was criticized for omitting the context

18   W. G. Sebald, *On the Natural History of Destruction*, New York: Modern Library Paperbacks, 2004.
19   Jörg Friedrich, *Freispruch für die Nazi-Justiz. Die Urteile gegen NS-Richter seit 1948. Eine Dokumentation*, Reinbeck: Rowohlt, 1983.
20   Jörg Friedrich, *Das Gesetz des Krieges. Das deutsche Heer in Russland 1941 bis 1945. Der Prozess gegen das Oberkommando der Wehrmacht*, Munich: Piper, 1993.

of Allied bombings, that of a war begun by Germany: was it right to focus historical analysis on the deliberate attack on German civilians and the sufferings they endured?

German historiography habitually emphasizes the fact that the first bombings of cities in the Second World War were the work of the Luftwaffe – those of Warsaw, Rotterdam, and Coventry having preceded the bombings of Hamburg and Dresden. Two remarks on this subject are needed. Another historiographic tradition, particularly in English language, has shown that this chronology, incontestable in itself, has only limited value. German military doctrine, long dominated by a conservative officer corps, recommended at the end of the First World War that aviation should be deployed tactically rather than strategically. Following the strategy of blitzkrieg, aircraft intervened in support of ground troops: something hardly surprising for a continental power that aimed to conquer territory rather than obtain a victory without occupation – the dream of strategic aviation. What is perhaps more surprising is the air doctrine adopted in 1936, already under the Nazi regime, that 'attack on cities with the aim of creating terror among the population must be rejected on principle'.[21] This of course did not exclude derogation from the rule, but it prevented emphasis on the construction of heavy bombers, a necessary condition for waging a true strategic campaign.

If it has been so hard to take these facts into account, this is quite simply because in the West, ever since 1945, the tendency has been to construct a historical narrative based on the opposition between liberal democracy and dictatorship,

---

21 Luftwaffendienstvorschrift 'Luftkriegsführung' (L.Dv. 16), Karl-Heinz Völker (ed.), *Dokumente und Dokumentarfotos zur Geschichte der deutschen Luftwaffe: Aus den Geheimakten des Reichswehrministeriums 1919–1933 und des Reichsluftfahrtministeriums 1933–1939*, Stuttgart: Deutsche Verlags-Anstalt, 1968, 482.

often assimilating fascism and Communism. Only recently has Nazism come increasingly to be understood not just as a mere pathology, but as a possibility inherent to the crisis of modernity.[22] This approach, moreover, allows comparisons to be made – something for a long time an absolute taboo – between democracies and fascist regimes, not to put them on the same level, but to understand possible convergences, potential contradictions, and differences in the industrial and nationalized societies of the twentieth century.[23]

Historiographic debate seems focused on the question of knowing whether the German civilian population can be viewed as victims of the Allied air war, or whether strategic bombing had been simply a response to German aggression, violent but necessary. The question of knowing 'who started it', Germans or British, is not only puerile, it also hides the real problems. First of all, as we have seen, the first aerial bomb was not dropped by either a German or a British pilot, but from an Italian plane in Libya. Then, it dispenses with historical analysis to substitute normative concerns. Perhaps what we need is neither apologies nor accusations, but simply clarity. Neither to laugh at strategic absurdities, nor to weep for those who died burned alive or asphyxiated, but to understand the profound political meaning of this manner of making war. Just like all strategic uses of aviation, the bombing campaign against Germany was guided by the 'democratic' hypothesis according to which the policy of a regime ultimately depends on the support of the people, in the double sense

---

22 See Michael Mann, *The Dark Side of Democracy: Explaining Ethnic Cleansing*, Cambridge: Cambridge University Press, 2004.

23 See for example Wolfgang Schivelbusch, *Three New Deals: Reflections on Roosevelt's America, Mussolini's Italy, and Hitler's Germany, 1933–1939*, New York: Picador, 2006.

of both collective sovereign and populace. In all logic, a British document of 1942 states that the primary aim of bombing should 'now be focussed on the morale of the enemy civil population and in particular, of the industrial workers'.[24] The object, in direct continuity with conceptions developed from the First World War, was to bomb the 'people' so that the industrial proletariat would exert its potential for social destabilization and thus bring about the collapse of the state. By its capacity to 'break up the whole social structure of the enemy in less than a week' (Giulio Douhet),[25] bombing was to reduce the 'people', sovereign and collective, to the state of an insurgent 'populace'.

As war involves a dialectic of defence and attack, so systems of anti-aircraft protection sought to counteract this objective. On the defensive side, therefore, the task was to strengthen social cohesion, to organize the 'populace' so as to constitute a homogeneous 'people', even if it necessarily remained structured by class, race, and gender. Making and unmaking a people – that is the alternative that sums up all strategic bombing. The Second World War in Europe provides a fascinating field of study for the way in which different political systems set about constructing the primordial political entity that is the 'people'. In this perspective, the most instructive examples are certainly those of the two great adversaries in the air war: Great Britain, archetype of liberal democracy, and Nazi Germany, the totalitarian society par excellence.[26]

---

24 '14th February 1942. Air Vice-Marshal N. H. Bottomley (Deputy Chief of the Air Staff) to Air Marshal J. E. A. Baldwin (acting air officer Commanding-in-Chief, Bomber Command)', in Charles Webster and Noble Frankland, *The Strategic Air Offensive Against Germany*, London: HMSO, 1954, vol. 4, 144.

25 Giulio Douhet, *The Command of the Air*, London: Faber and Faber, 1943, 14.

26 The following paragraphs draw above all on two comparative

Reflecting the militarization of civilian life, the microcosm of the air-raid shelter perfectly crystallized the attitudes, both collective and individual, adopted in a society at war, the imaginaries of nation and people, the conflicts and tensions, micro-powers, norms, and resistances.[27] The bunker was the necessary complement to the systems of social security and national integration that were indispensable to the creation of a sense of 'social justice', a pillar of the 'morale' of the population on the 'home front'. Whether massive urban monuments or buried beneath the ground, shelters were the materialization of the ideas that were made of the people, and access to these places concretely showed who was part of the national community, on what grounds and on what conditions.[28]

In both Great Britain and Germany, discipline, obedience, and the struggle against fires were all part of the organization of life in the face of air attacks. Carrying out one's duty, being ready for sacrifice, showing solidarity with companions in misfortune, having 'trust' in the state –

studies of these two countries: Bernd Lemke, *Luftschutz in Grossbritannien und Deutschland 1923 bis 1939: Zivile Kriegsvorbereitungen als Ausdruck der Staats-und gesellschaftspolitischen Grundlagen von Demokratie und Diktatur*, Munich: Oldenbourg, 2005, and in particular the excellent work of Dietmar Süss, *Death From the Skies*, especially chapters 2 and 6.

27 Sources for these are the reports of Mass Observation for Great Britain, and for Nazi Germany the *Lageberichte* of the SS Sicherheitsdienst. For Mass Observation, see Charles Madge and Tom Harrison, *Britain by Mass Observation*, Harmondsworth: Penguin, 1939. For the *Lageberichte*, see Heinz Boberach, 'Einleitung', in *Meldungen aus dem Reich. Auswahl aus den geheimen Lageberichten des Sicherheitsdienstes der SS 1939–1944*, Neuwied-Berlin: Luchterhand, 1965, ix–xxviii.

28 See Bernd Lemke, 'Zivile Kriegsvorbereitungen in unterschiedlichen Staats- und Gesellschaftssystemen. Der Luftschutz im 20. Jahrhundert – ein Überblick', in Bernd Lemke (ed.), *Luft- und Zivilschutz in Deutschland im 20. Jahrhundert*, Potsdam: Militärgeschichtliches Forschungsamt, 2007, 67–88.

such were the virtues essential for standing firm under the bombs. In this set-up, control of fear was indispensable for stabilizing social relations that were threatened with dissolution. Shelters, conceived in both countries as places that were eminently political, focused all kinds of social conflict and were marked by a dialectic between organization directed by the state, on the one hand, and social self-organization on the other. In Germany, the tension between state bodies and those of the Nazi Party, typical of many totalitarian regimes, made itself felt in the management of shelters. While air-raid protection was coordinated by the air ministry, the 'political task' of managing shelters, controlling access to them and maintaining morale, discipline, and order within them, was entrusted to a *Bunkerwart*, appointed not by the ministry but rather by the party, and who accordingly represented the *Volksgemeinschaft* as a whole, this racialized 'community of the people'. The *Bunkerwart* had sovereign prerogatives: deciding on admission, he held the right to preserve life in the shelter or let people die in the flames. His British counterpart was the 'shelter warden', appointed by the police. Often recruited from local shopkeepers, the shelter wardens were supposed to support morale by showing themselves affable, helpful, and understanding. In practice, however, they also possessed an immense power over the shelter, and thus over people's lives, which gave them, in the expression of one Londoner, 'a huge opportunity for little Hitlering'.[29] The shelter could thus easily mutate into a micro-fascist system.

The most obvious difference between German and British shelters concerned the racialization of the national community. Theoretically, in Germany, only Aryans had a right to protection, but an Air Ministry circular of October

---

29 Tom Harrison, *Living Through the Blitz*, London: Collins, 1976, 120, quoted by Süss, *Death From the Skies*, 314.

1940 spelled out that access should not be completely refused to Jews, for fear that they might profit from an air raid to burgle deserted apartments. Separate shelters were also established for Jews and Aryans. If this problem came to an end with the massive deportations, it immediately shifted to other racialized categories: prisoners of war and forced labourers from Eastern Europe – forbidden access to the shelters – as well as other foreigners, particularly Italians but also French – who could be admitted if space allowed. This explains why those excluded from the national community were largely over-represented among the victims of bombing: the 'non-Aryan' forced labourer was far more likely than a German to perish under the bombs that were supposed to free him.[30]

As expressions of the new national community to be cemented, German bunkers were often built on the sites of former synagogues. The racialized *Volksgemeinschaft* was literally built on the destruction of its other. It was quite coherent, then, that contemporaries should perceive a dialectical relationship between the bombing and the Judeocide: a Hamburg shopkeeper wrote in a letter that

> despite all the anger against the English and Americans, on account of their inhumane manner of waging war, it has to be quite objectively noted that ordinary people, the middle classes and other circles, often make remarks, in private and even in company, that see the attacks as reprisals against the treatment we are inflicting on the Jews.[31]

This relationship, however, which here takes the form of a feeling of deserved collective punishment, also worked in the opposite direction: many letters sent to the authorities

30 Ibid., 309–10.
31 Ibid., 99.

asked them to 'make the Jews pay' for the 'war crimes' committed by the Allies, and present the gas chambers as a response to 'Anglo-American air terror'.[32]

In Great Britain, on the other hand, the ambiguities of national integration were crystallized in the concept of 'people's war'.[33] Here, although access to shelters was clearly not based on any racial regulation, certain categories, and 'the Jews' in particular, nonetheless found themselves stigmatized for their 'egoism' and lack of solidarity or discipline. A policeman declared in October 1940, for example, that 95 per cent of those who occupied the overcrowded Oxford Circus shelter in central London were German Jews and not really English.[34] Jews were also held responsible for the chaotic scenes often produced at the entrance to shelters. In both countries, access to air-raid protection was not an unconditional civil right: it was officially subordinated to commitment to a community and adhesion to its values. 'Britishness' was also defined in relation to a racialized 'other', but contrary to what happened under the Nazi regime, British democracy offered possibilities of integration: Jews could become members of the national community, on condition that they adapted to 'British values' and made the effort to 'integrate'[35] – which amounted to viewing them as themselves responsible for the exclusion to which they were subject.

As distinct from race relations, sexual relations were

---

32   Ibid., 100.

33   See in particular Angus Calder, *The People's War: Britain, 1939–1945*. Also Sonya O. Rose, *Which People's War? National Identity and Citizenship in Wartime Britain, 1939–1945*, Oxford: Oxford University Press, 2004.

34   Süss, *Death From the Skies*, 315.

35   Tony Kushner, *The Persistence of Prejudice: Antisemitism in British Society during the Second World War*, Manchester: Manchester University Press, 1989, 197.

remarkably similar in the shelters of both countries.[36] This was quite simply because women were the pillar of the community. In Germany, they enjoyed privileged access to shelters, whereas men aged from sixteen to sixty were officially excluded. According to the established division of tasks, man was supposed to fight while woman kept the family home, and by extension the national one. It was women, therefore, who were the object of official recommendations as to the behaviour to adopt in case of alarm. Since they were supposed to be less stable than men, management of their fear constituted a political challenge of the utmost importance – for which reason they had to be directed by a *Bunkerwart* or shelter warden, necessarily male. However, many testimonies of soldiers who underwent bombing while at home on leave show that the fear felt in the shelters was far greater than what they experienced on the front. Not only was it harder to be subjected to bombing without having the possibility of response, but this passivity, difficult to reconcile with warlike and masculine virtues, exposed them to symbolic castration. At all events, male suffering was habitually ignored. Attention focused above all on women, who were the object of a paradoxical attention. By their virtue, they held together the community, but by their femininity (and thus their weakness), they represented a threat of mental and social dissolution. They thus found themselves in a dual position, comparable to that of the 'people', at the same time sovereign and 'populace'. This is why the threat arising from gender was most often indissociable from that presented by the lower social classes.

---

36 See Nicole Kramer, '"Kämpfende Mütter" und "gefallene Heldinnen" – Frauen im Luftschutz', in Dietmar Süss (ed.), *Deutschland im Luftkrieg. Geschichte und Erinnerung*, Munich: Oldenbourg, 2007, 85–98.

As spaces of promiscuous proximity, often lit poorly if at all, where existential fear suddenly was converted to the euphoria of being still alive and no longer having anything to lose, bunkers were also places of uncontrolled sexual encounters. The concern to discipline sexual conduct seems to have played a greater role in Great Britain than in Nazi Germany. Contrary to an idea born in the 1950s, according to which Nazism was marked by sexual repression, the anti-bourgeois dimension of the *Volksgemeinschaft* implied certain possibilities of sexual liberation.[37] The British 'people's war', on the other hand, was based far more strongly on a community founded on the bourgeois family and the need to repress sexual deviance, imputable both to women and the lower orders. As a clear sign of the particular role played by the family, the British authorities were initially against the idea of collective shelters, fearing that, in this mixing of classes, bourgeois virtue might be contaminated by the bad habits of the 'lower orders', leading to moral dissolution followed by a challenge to the social order. The middle classes were thus encouraged to build shelters in their gardens, which had the additional advantage of privatizing part of the costs bound up with air-raid precautions – something unthinkable in Germany, where the collective ideology of the *Volksgemeinschaft* was paramount.[38]

The population gathered in the shelters was largely made up of proletarians, to the great irritation of the middle class when they were forced to rub shoulders. The Berlin journalist Ursula von Kardorff, for example, described a 'horde

---

37 Dagmar Herzog, *Sex After Fascism: Memory and Morality in Twentieth-Century Germany*, Princeton: Princeton University Press, 2005, especially 59.
38 For a literary treatment of this question, see the novel by Helmut Krauser, *Eros*, New York: Europa Editions, 2008.

of human animals' who took refuge in a shelter, a real pressure cooker that only the presence of the forces of order prevented from exploding.[39] The bourgeois perception of life in the shelters was the exact reflection of the assumptions of air strategy – the 'populace' would explode the social order guaranteed by the state – or, what amounted to the same thing, military strategy was informed by a bourgeois view of politics.

The test of the war presented both Germany and Great Britain with the same challenge: to consolidate national and social integration in a capitalist system organized by the state. The results were necessarily ambiguous, inasmuch as the actual tendency towards more or less egalitarian integration[40] was always combined with the persistence of class antagonism.[41] We can rather schematically maintain nonetheless that the *Volksgemeinschaft* tended more towards the imaginary of an egalitarian society, imposed with unprecedented violence in order to camouflage existing inequalities and to physically eliminate all that resisted it, whether practically or symbolically. The 'people's war', on the other hand, had greater difficulty in articulating the integration of the working class with an imaginary of the nation that was deeply bourgeois, in which 'Britishness'

---

39 Süss, *Death From the Skies*, 315.

40 For Germany, see the classic study by Martin Broszat, 'Soziale Motivation und Führer-Bindung des Nationalsozialismus', *Vierteljahreshefte für Zeitgeschichte*, 18 (1970), 392–409; for Great Britain, Rodney Lowe, 'The Second World War, Consensus, and the Foundation of the Welfare State', *20th Century British History*, 1 (1990), 152–82, as well as Calder, *The People's War*.

41 For Nazi Germany, see in particular Timothy W. Mason, *Nazism, Fascism and the Working Class*, Cambridge: Cambridge University Press, 1995; for Great Britain, Robert Mackays, *Half the Battle: Civilian Morale in Britain during the Second World War*, Manchester: Manchester University Press, 2003, and Rose, *Which People's War?*

combined sangfroid and dry humour, eccentricity and sense of order, politeness in social life and bravery in war.[42] In Great Britain, shelters were often condemned as gathering places for social parasites who shamelessly profited from the help provided by the state, instead of taking responsibility for themselves in an independent and responsible fashion.[43] The shelter thus aroused critique of a liberal kind, which viewed the social state as a guardian that deprived people of responsibility. At the other end of the political spectrum, the moderate left viewed shelters as a foretaste of the social-democratic paradise. The journalist Richard Calder gave underground life in London an oriental coloration: '[B]lack and white, brown and yellow, men from the Levant and Slavs from Eastern Europe; Jew, Gentile, Moslem and Hindu' mingled peacefully and rubbed shoulders with prostitutes, soldiers, pilots, sailors, and criminals. The success – and scandal – of Calder's reports bore on the fact that this strange and foreign world seemed suddenly very close: the East no longer began in Cairo, but at Oxford Circus. Perhaps more important than the racial medley, Calder uses this backdrop of eastern hybridization to describe forms of democratic self-organization located below the established power of the state. We thus see former hoodlums transformed into responsible citizens who not only obey the collective rules, but also show solidarity and mutual respect, helping each other to bridge racial and social barriers.[44] What is particularly significant is that this 'upside-down' world of the shelter immediately found itself targeted by the authorities,

42 On 'Britishness', see Linda Colley, *Britons, Forging the Nation 1707–1837*, London: Yale University Press, 1992, also Robert Colls and Phillip Dodd (eds), *Englishness: Politics and Culture 1880–1920*, London: Croom Helm, 1987.
43 Süss, *Death From the Skies*, 318.
44 Ibid., 305.

who, rather than taking advantage of the possibilities offered by this form of autonomous community organizing, saw it as the subversive work of 'Jews' and 'Communists'.

As a microcosm that contains all the virtual possibilities of the national-social capitalist state system of the twentieth century, the air-raid shelter could also generate the utopia of a multiculturalism backed up by welfare, with a stronger or weaker dose of economic and social liberalism, reflecting that of a totalitarian or fascist society. It was precisely that protean character of nationalized modern societies that George Orwell described in 1941, at the start of his essay 'The Lion and the Unicorn':

> As I write, highly civilized human beings are flying overhead, trying to kill me. They do not feel any enmity against me as an individual, nor I against them ... Most of them, I have no doubt, are kind-hearted law-abiding men who would never dream of committing murder in private life. On the other hand, if one of them succeeds in blowing me to pieces with a well-placed bomb, he will never sleep any the worse for it.[45]

---

45   George Orwell, 'The Lion and the Unicorn', in *The Collected Essays, Journalism and Letters of George Orwell*, vol. 2, *My Country Right or Left*, Harmondsworth: Penguin, 1970, 74.

CHAPTER 9

'Revolutionary War' beneath
the Nuclear Shield

His hysterical shouts become incontrollable. He screams, swears, curses, gesticulates like a madman. 'Bullshit. Just, just, just cream the fuckers!'[1] Each word is emphasized with a fist on the table. 'The point is, we're not going to go out whimpering, and we're not going to go out losing ... I'm gonna knock their goddamn brains out ... I'm, we're gonna take out the dikes, we're gonna take out the power plants, we're gonna take out Haiphong, we're gonna level that goddamn country!'[2]

Mr President –

Now that makes me shout.

Mr President, I will enthusiastically support that, and I think it's the right thing to do ... Mr President, there's two, there's one other thing you can say – before you get to that part of it – you can say, first of all, your record proves that you, uh; that, uh you have reduced those operations that you can. There's no bombing, there's practically no bombing going on in South Vietnam anymore. Eighty-five per cent of the bombing is in the uninhabited areas of Laos! These people talk as if we're slaughtering civilians.[3]

---

1   Quoted in Jeffrey Kimball, *The Vietnam War Files: Uncovering the Secret History of Nixon-Era Strategy*, Lawrence: University Press of Kansas, 2004, 146.
2   Ibid., 159.
3   Ibid., 163.

'Operation Linebacker', as titled by President Nixon and his national security adviser Henry Kissinger, lasted from May to October 1972, and would be the most massive bombing campaign in the history of air warfare. In six months, the United States dropped almost 7 million tons of bombs on Vietnam, more than five times what the Allies had dropped on Germany during the Second World War. Twenty-six million bombs shredded the soil of the country, which at the time had between 35 and 40 million inhabitants. The scale of human losses is impossible to assess precisely. On the lowest estimates these were up to 1.3 million, while others estimate the number of victims among Vietnamese combatants at 1 million, out of a total of 2 million killed and 4 million wounded. It is likewise impossible to know how many civilians perished, but one thing is sure: the proportion of civilian victims was particularly high, between 46 and 66 per cent.

Operation 'Linebacker II', also called the 'Christmas bombings', took place from 18 to 29 December 1972. Its express aim was to strike the morale of the civilian populations of Hanoi and Haiphong – only 12 per cent of the attacks aimed at military targets. 'Now there's nothing more to lose. Nothing. We'll hit them, bomb them, exterminate them!' we hear Nixon shout in the Oval Office.[4] This political line decided in the White House was soon translated into military terms. The air force general Curtis LeMay had long argued for a still more massive use of bombing: 'My solution to the problem would be to tell them frankly that they've got to draw in their horns and stop their aggression or we're going to bomb them back into the Stone Age with airpower or naval power – not with ground forces.'[5]

---

4   Ibid.
5   Bill Yenne, *Strategic Air Command: A Primer of Modern Strategic Air Power*, London: Arms & Armour Press, 1984, 86.

The Vietnam war was particularly deadly, as it fell at the intersection of two genealogical lines of twentieth-century warfare: 'asymmetrical' conflict in the tradition of colonial wars, with their potentially limitless violence; and conflict overdetermined by the specific global configuration of the Cold War. The Vietnamese defined their struggle as one of 'national liberation', conceiving it after the European model of the construction of a nation state. As for the United States, they saw the anticolonial aspiration to self-determination as a feint designed to camouflage Soviet and Chinese expansionism: behind the Viet Cong stood the Kremlin with its tanks and missiles. The guerrillas were part of the Communist bloc, embodied by a state that was itself perceived as monolithic.[6]

In sum, there was an odd combination of symmetry and asymmetry in the perceptions of the two adversaries, and the Vietnam War combined the worst of two traditions: that of total war between nation states, and that of the 'small war' of insurrectionary or colonial type. These contradictory tendencies – statization and fragmentation – continue to characterize the conflicts that haunt us today. Moreover, the importance of this war for the development of the US army's strategic doctrine cannot be overstated. For all these reasons, the Vietnam War constitutes a fundamental link in the genealogy of twentieth-century warfare.

The US military leaders drew a conclusion from the Second World War that was both deeply rooted and mistaken: according to them, aviation had been the key agent of victory. The reasons for this misinterpretation are many, and partly connected with a situation of inter-service rivalry, in which a very large share of the defence budget

---

6   Marc J. Selverstone, *Constructing the Monolith: The United States, Great Britain, and International Communism, 1945–1950*, Cambridge, MA: Harvard University Press, 2009.

was allocated to an air force that had not yet acquired institutional independence. To present aviation as the decisive factor of victory was thus, as we saw, a way for the USAF to better position itself vis-à-vis other branches of the armed forces. It is clear that the atom bomb helped fuel the imaginary of aerial omnipotence. For the state, the most important question was to justify the exorbitant cost of the 'Manhattan project', explaining that not only had nuclear weapons played a key role in the war that had just ended, but that they would also be in future the pillar of US defence policy. Finally, in strategic terms, nuclear weapons fitted perfectly into the framework of Douhetism that was then hegemonic in the Anglo-Saxon world, the atom bomb being simply a larger bomb than any other.

After the war, US defence policy was thus essentially focused on the combination of nuclear weapons and aviation. In 1945 the Strategic Air Command was established and became the nerve centre of the US military system: 'The Strategic Air Command is the soul of our defence,' said Thomas Finletter, secretary of state for the air force.[7] This orientation was further strengthened under Eisenhower's presidency. Because of budget constraints, the 'New Look' strategists believed that nuclear weapons were the only way of responding to threat: they should be used anywhere in the world, against any initiative that impinged on US interests.[8] This doctrine was clearly based on the mistaken assumption of a 'Communist bloc' that was homogeneous in all respects, and whose ardour could only be inflected by pressure on the Kremlin.

---

7   Quoted by Camille Rougeron, *Les Enseignements de la guerre de Corée*, Paris: Berger-Levrault, 1952, 188.

8   Robert R. Bowie and Richard H. Immerman, *Waging Peace: How Eisenhower Shaped an Enduring Cold War Strategy*, Oxford: Oxford University Press, 1997.

Although this policy became considerably more flexible under Kennedy, it still weighed heavily on the military apparatus at the time of the Vietnam War. Maxwell D. Taylor, author of a thorough critique of the 'New Look'[9] who was appointed chief of the general staff by the new president, sought from the early 1960s to rebalance US strategy by rehabilitating the concept of 'limited war', placing the concept of 'flexible response' at the centre of his analysis. The idea was to escape the strategic trap intrinsic to Douhetism and the nuclear strategy of the 1950s; it was certainly possible to destroy the world, but not to win a real war. According to the New Look strategy, centred on strategic aviation and nuclear weapons, the United States represented a potentially immense threat to any adversary; yet it seemed hardly credible that it would embark on a nuclear war for such a limited goal as countering the national liberation movements in what was then called the 'Third World'. For this reason, from the 1960s US strategy would consist in defending limited interests by limited wars, below the threshold of global nuclear war. The 'response' now had to be 'flexible', which also meant unpredictable for the adversary. This unpredictability also lay at the centre of the 'madman' theory proclaimed by Nixon, who saw it as useful for the world to imagine a US president mad enough to risk the very existence of the planet for the sake of his anti-Communist obsession. The dialectic immortalized by Stanley Kubrick in *Dr Strangelove* – that of the total unpredictability of the madman theory and its opposite, the automatic triggering of nuclear weapons – thus had a very real strategic foundation.

Unpredictability was combined with a further strategic requirement, that of credibility. The whole world had to

---

9 Maxwell D. Taylor, *The Uncertain Trumpet*, London: Atlantic Books, 1960.

understand that the United States was ready to defend its interests, however limited and located in distant regions, and that it would not let down its allies. If the message sent from the Vietnam jungle was addressed to the world as a whole, it was also addressed to the 'home front' of American society, which had to be mobilized for this type of war of intervention. According to Defence Secretary Robert McNamara,

> the greatest contribution Vietnam is making ... is developing an ability in the United States to fight a limited war, to go to war without arousing the public ire ... because this is the kind of war we'll likely be facing for the next fifty years.[10]

These developments explain to a certain degree why the Americans did not draw the lessons of the French defeats in Indochina and Algeria. Despite these precedents, which suggested that aviation could at best play only a very secondary role in this type of conflict, they deployed tremendous military and aviation resources in Vietnam, including the heaviest bombers, the mythical B-52s, built for intercontinental strategic bombing against the Soviet Union and quite unsuited for guerrilla warfare in the jungle.

As for the Vietnamese Communists, their strategy was based on two pillars: a guerrilla war waged in the south of the country, and control of the state in the north. Their combat closely followed Mao Zedong's precepts on 'revolutionary war', which has three successive phases: defence, equilibrium, and offensive.[11] The first phase, strategic defence, is dedicated to the construction and strengthening

---

10 Quoted by Bernd Greiner, *War without Fronts: The USA in Vietnam*, London: Bodley Head, 2009, 66.

11 Mao Tse-tung, 'Problems of Strategy in China's Revolutionary War', in *Selected Works of Mao Tse-tung*, Peking: Foreign Languages Press, 1967, vol. 1, 179–254.

of the party: recruiting new members, initially from the margins of society rather than from among the 'masses', placing cadres in key positions at the local level, getting the party identified with popular causes, such as agrarian reform, in order to win the affection of the population.

The second phase, that of equilibrium, corresponds to guerrilla warfare: conducting sabotage operations, establishing parallel administrations in 'liberated' areas, but also placing demands on the civilian population, with a view to intimidating 'neutrals' and forcing them to support the insurgents. In this second phase, civilians are deliberately taken hostage and held in a vice between the colonial power and the Maoist rebels. The point for the latter is to rally the population to their cause by recourse, on the one hand, to a mixture of proto-welfare and nationalism, and on the other hand, to terror, for example by forcing the population to provide them with assistance, so as to trigger reprisals which will in turn increase the sentiment that their only salvation can come from revolution and national liberation. This strategy was an integral part of the strategy of 'revolutionary war'. Between 1957 and 1972, the Viet Cong killed at least 37,000 Vietnamese suspected of supporting the enemy, and kidnapped at least 58,000 persons for various political reasons, particularly to send the political signal that neither the US forces nor the Saigon government could protect them.[12]

The third and final phase is that of an almost conventional war. Until the end of the conflict, the Vietnamese political and military leaders continued to believe that they were still in the second phase, while remaining determined to abandon the guerrilla strategy when the right moment came (which clearly shows that their political perspective

---

12 Greiner, *War without Fronts*, 33.

was that of a nation state with a monopoly of violence). The rare attempts to launch large-scale operations, such as the Têt offensive in early 1968, which approached conventional warfare, met with military defeat for the insurgents, who learned to their cost that they could not win a conventional war against a US army with crushing superiority. But the main lesson of the Vietnam War was that it was not necessary to seek to obtain victory in the classic sense of the term.

In an asymmetrical conflict, time inexorably works in favour of the weaker party, who 'wins' as long as the enemy does not triumph. For this it must be prepared to accept considerable losses at every level: 'the [Vietnam Communist] Party has been guided by the principle that it is better to kill ten innocent people than to let one enemy escape.'[13] To be clear: it was acceptable for ten Vietnamese to perish against a single US soldier killed. In the same logic, the insurgents launched attacks from inhabited zones, which incited the United States to bomb their villages by way of response. At the height of their power, the Viet Cong counted close to 200,000 fighters and more than 40,000 auxiliaries; while between 1964 and 1974, they lost at least 440,000 soldiers, amounting to twice the total strength of their army. The number of US troops killed was 56,000 – if the sacrifice had been equivalent on both sides, then a million American soldiers would not have returned home.

Losses of this scale are an integral part of the strategy of revolutionary war, the insurgents being convinced that they are strong enough to endure such blows. Not only were such sacrifices accepted, they were even seen by many anticolonial leaders as desirable, the necessary means for

---

13   Ibid., 38.

cementing a national people made up of former colonized subjects. The most remarkable formulation in this respect was in fact offered by the apostle of non-violence Mahatma Gandhi, who declared in 1942 that a million deaths were needed in order for India to become a viable nation:

> [I]t would be a good thing if a million people were shot in a brave and non-violent rebellion against British rule. It may be that it may take us years before we can evolve order out of chaos. But we can then face the world. We cannot face the world today. Avowedly the different nations are fighting for their liberty. Germany, Japan, Russia, China are pouring their blood and money like water. What is *our* record? ... We are betraying a woeful cowardice. I do not mind the blood-bath in which Europe is plunged. It is bad enough, but there is a great deal of heroism – mothers losing their only children, wives their husbands and so on.[14]

On the other hand, the Vietnamese guerrilla forces correctly believed that American society's spirit of sacrifice was limited, given that the country's vital interests were not at stake. To sum up, the insurgents banked on two factors: time and the escalation of violence. They could well sacrifice a large section of their population, and two entire armies, yet they would win as long as the enemy had not succeeded in eliminating them politically. In the good old tradition of guerrilla warfare, going back at least to the Napoleonic Wars, the insurgents had recourse to forms of extreme violence, often highly ritualized: GIs caught in ambush were often tortured, and their mutilated

---

14 M. K. Gandhi, 'Interview to Journalist', *Harijan*, 2 August 1942, in *Collected Works of Mahatma Gandhi*, 1979, vol. 76, 329, quoted in Faisal Devji, *The Impossible Indian: Gandhi and the Temptations of Violence*, London: Hurst, 2012, 155.

bodies exposed publicly – flayed, gutted, and castrated. The American rear was vulnerable, Colonel Bui Tin explained: 'The conscience of America was part of its war-making capability, and we were turning that power in our favour. America lost because of its democracy; through dissent and protest it lost the ability to mobilize a will to win.'[15]

This strategy amounted to a considerable challenge for the stronger side in such a conflict. Conscious that time was working against them, and that they could only win rapidly, the US policymakers mobilized ever greater forces with the hope of crushing the insurgents. According to William DePuy, head of US military operations, 'the solution in Vietnam is more bombs, more shells, more napalm ... till the other side cracks and gives up'.[16] At the same time, the configuration of the Cold War and the threat of nuclear war also imposed restrictions. There could be no question of invading North Vietnam to cut off the insurgents in the South from their source of supply, as the risk of direct confrontation with China was too great, especially in a situation where the intentions of the Soviet Union did not seem clear.

The United States was thus confined to bombing the north of the country with a 'coercive' aim while seeking to 'pacify' the south. Aviation played a preponderant role on both fronts. 'Coercive bombing' meant the strategy of imposing one's will on the enemy by inflicting unsustainable losses and threatening him with still greater ones.[17] It is readily understandable why such a strategy has no chance of success vis-à-vis an enemy whose entire strategy pre-

15   'How North Vietnam Won the War', interview with Colonel Bui Tin, *Wall Street Journal*, 3 August 1995, quoted by Greiner, *War without Fronts*, 37.
16   Quoted by Greiner, *War without Fronts*, 55.
17   Thomas C. Schelling, *The Strategy of Conflict*, Cambridge, MA: Harvard University Press, 1960.

cisely involves the acceptance of losses, even colossal ones. Apart from institutional and doctrinal reasons specific to the military machine, the US stubbornness in continuing on a path doomed to failure in advance is attributable above all to reasons of domestic policy.

In 1972, faced with a public opinion that was increasingly hostile to the war, all candidates in the upcoming presidential election promised to put a speedy end to the conflict. And contrary to popular belief, there were few illusions in Washington about the real situation in Vietnam: the political leaders knew that sooner or later the United States would lose the war. Starting from this premise, three political solutions presented themselves: first of all, send more troops in the hope of winning regardless, and winning quickly; second, postponing the decision until later, which amounted to continuing the war so as to delay defeat; and third, withdraw without having obtained the political results in the name of which the United States had embarked on this conflict, which amounted to accepting a defeat. No president had the political courage to choose this third 'solution', and the strategic bombing campaign increasingly followed the logic of the second. In scarcely veiled terms, accordingly, Nixon said that the objective of his 'Linebacker' campaign was to give the Saigon government a 'decent interval', which clearly meant that the inevitable collapse of South Vietnam should not take place before his re-election in November 1972 or, still better, not before the projected end of his mandate four years later.[18]

It was the second 'front', however, that of 'pacification' in the south, that saw the most significant developments in the air war on Vietnam. Ever since the First World War, strategic and tactical deployment of aviation had been

---

18   Greiner, *War without Fronts*, 53.

distinguished, the first being directed predominantly against civilian populations and the second against armed forces. In guerrilla warfare, however, this distinction tended to blur.[19] Such tactical operations as 'close support' in an inhabited milieu inevitably killed a large number of civilians. More fundamentally, the United States pursued a strategy of 'attrition' in which strategic success was supposed to come from the sum of tactical successes. Instead of seeking to 'bend the will' of the enemy, the attempt was to physically eliminate a maximum of insurgents and cut off the survivors from their bases of support. As far as the latter point was concerned, the United States drew on French and British doctrines, developed in Indochina, Algeria, and Malaya, which consisted in the transfer of large sections of the population, the creation of theoretically uninhabited 'free-fire zones', and the relocation of civilians in 'strategic hamlets' or fortified villages, surrounded with barbed wire, under strict surveillance and cut off from any contact with the insurgents.

The other element in the attrition strategy, which was to kill as many insurgents as possible, was translated into operational reality with the concept of 'meat-grinder', which, according to General William Westmoreland, had the aim of decimating the Vietnamese population 'to the point of national disaster for generations to come',[20] as well as by the tactic of 'search and destroy', which meant using airborne troops, generally sent in by helicopter, to intervene in enemy territory in order to find and massacre the insurgents before rapidly departing. In practice, this meant attacking villages or hamlets where presumed

---

19   Patrick Facon, *Le Bombardement stratégique*, Monaco: Le Rocher, 1996, 269.
20   Joe Allen, *Vietnam: The (Last) War the U.S. Lost*, Chicago: Haymarket Books, 2008, 39.

insurgents or their sympathizers were hiding. Added to this were the effect of the 'Phoenix programme', conceived after the French counter-revolutionary doctrine developed in the wake of the Indochina war and applied in Algeria.[21] The objective here was to identify and 'neutralize' the leading cadres of the revolutionary organization: infiltration, arrest, torture, and assassination.

The Vietnam War was thus the laboratory of a technique of government already tested during the Second World War, which steadily invaded all spheres of society: 'benchmarking', in other words the use of numerical indicators to improve performance. In the attrition strategy deployed in Vietnam, the benchmark was the 'body count', the number of enemies killed per week by each unit. Enormous pressure was placed on the commanders, who subsequently transmitted this to their subordinates – the effects are not hard to imagine. Whether in the context of the Phoenix programme or in simple 'search and destroy' missions, commandos systematically attacked villages or hamlets by helicopter, in such a way that the famous scene from the film *Apocalypse Now*, which shows an attack to the music of Wagner's 'Ride of the Valkyries', does not seem that far from historical reality.

In theory, the real mission began on the ground, after a helicopter attack. If there was a Viet Cong response, artillery or bomber planes were brought in: 'I could … within an hour get a B-52 strike destroying an entire grid square [one square kilometre] on a map, and we did that',[22] one officer recalled. If there was no response, troops criss-

---

21 On the French strategy of 'revolutionary war', see Mathieu Rigouste, *L'Ennemi intérieur: la généalogie coloniale et militaire de l'ordre sécuritaire dans la France contemporaine*, Paris: La Découverte, 2009.

22 Greiner, *War without Fronts*, 62.

crossed the ground. Sometimes only armed men or other suspects were arrested; at other times, all the inhabitants were taken to 'interrogation centres'. According to one US soldier who described these missions, 'we know they're Charlie [Viet Cong] – maybe saboteurs, collaborators, and like that ... These here are hard-core V.C. You can tell by lookin' at 'em.'[23] About 220,000 persons were arrested in this way, more than a quarter of them classified as 'civilian defendants', presumed to be spies, saboteurs, terrorists, or collaborators.

These suspects were very likely to be tortured, either in the jails of the Saigon regime or on US bases. A Red Cross report of 1968–69 records torture by electricity or water, sexual humiliation, beatings, mutilation, dehydration, imprisonment with pythons or in small barbed-wire cages. According to the US general Edward Bautz, torture was a military necessity and thus an everyday practice, and the chief of staff Harold K. Johnson even admitted that the treatment of the Viet Cong captured by the Americans was worse than that of GIs who fell into enemy hands.[24] An original technique practised by US troops was 'airborne interrogation', which consisted in throwing prisoners selected at random out of helicopters, in order to terrorize others.

Practices of this kind inevitably went together with an image of the enemy based largely on 'Orientalist' stereotypes. According to US General Peers, charged with investigating the massacre of 350 to 500 Vietnamese civilians at My Lai in March 1968, the attitude of the incriminated soldiers towards the Vietnamese was 'the most disturbing characteristic' of these events. 'You can't realize what they are thinking. They seem to have no under-

---

23   Ibid., 76.
24   Ibid., 79–80.

standing of life. They don't care whether they live or die.'[25] The Vietnamese became the absolute 'other': 'It doesn't matter what you do to them ... The trouble is no one sees the Vietnamese as people ... even if when a Vietnamese guy speaks perfect English I don't know what the hell he's talking about.'[26] Since Vietnam was a permanent threat, all its inhabitants indifferently became enemies to be killed: 'They're all V-C or at least helping them – same difference. You can't convert them, only kill them. Don't lose any sleep over those dead children – they grow up to be commies too.'[27]

The asymmetrical strategy saw the disappearance not only of the symmetry that characterized the 'just enemy' in Europe, but also of the very possibility of acknowledging the other's humanity. Churchill still believed that one could 'treat' a part of the German population. This did not apply to the Vietnamese. They could not be 'treated' and converted to the just cause, they could only be killed. The same premise applied even to children, thus to future generations, which was close to the traditional racism based on the very 'nature' of the enemy population. These perceptions were thus the reflection of a colonial and racist imaginary that had long been attached to aviation, and in many respects the Vietnam War did indeed follow the pattern of colonial wars with an exterminatory aim. The American journalist David Halberstam even said that in Vietnam 'we were fighting the birthrate of a nation'.[28] In this war, too, it was the 'people' who became the principal

---

25 Richard Hammer, 'Interviews with My Lai Veterans', *Evergreen*, n.d., 56, quoted in Greiner, *War without Fronts*, 125.
26 Ibid., 80.
27 Ibid., 84.
28 Quoted in David L. Anderson (ed.), *Facing My Lai: Moving Beyond the Massacre*, Lawrence: University Press of Kansas, 1998, 132.

target, but in a sense slightly different from that which could be observed in the traditional colonial wars and in the total war in Europe.

In revolutionary war of Maoist inspiration, as already in the 'insurrectionary war' championed by Engels's 'Prussian irregulars' – Gneisenau, Scharnhorst, and Clausewitz – the centre of gravity was nowhere else but in the people.[29] The object of an irregular, insurrectionary, revolutionary war is essentially to win the political support of the population. Conversely, regular armies have long sought to integrate into their 'counter-insurrectionary' doctrines the fact that a war of this kind cannot be won without the support of the people. The insurgents have every interest in appearing as an emanation of the people, as this also enables them to define who is part of this people and who, on the contrary, deserves to be brought before a revolutionary tribunal as an 'enemy of the people'. In a movement of reciprocal defi-nition, the insurgents *are* the people, in and for itself, both its purest emanation and the power that establishes it.

The people also lay at the heart of the approach of the United States as a great power. The campaigns of strategic bombing against North Vietnam followed the same logic as those at work during total war, whereas in the counter-insurrectionary war waged in the south, everything had to be done to separate the insurgents from the people and present them as mere 'terrorists' lacking a popular base. That was precisely the objective of the transfers of popula-tions to strategic hamlets. As a result, the intervening power loses the war if it falls into the trap set by the insurgents, and contributes to assimilating the latter with the people

---

29 On the Prussian concepts of insurrectionary war and *Volk-skrieg* in the early nineteenth century, see Thomas Hippler, *Soldats et citoyens: naissance du service militaire en France et en Prussie*, Paris: PUF, 2006.

as such. Once the counter-insurrection forces are perceived as waging a war against the people and not just against the insurgents, the latter have in fact won the political battle. This is precisely why it is possible to speak, and not only in relation to Vietnam, of an objective alliance between insurgents and counter-insurrection forces: when both entities are fighting for the people, the population inevitably pays the price.

Although the legacy of colonial war clearly affected the conduct of operations in Vietnam, it would be wrong to underestimate their novelty, which is immediately apparent when the American war is compared with that of the French in the same theatre. In both Indochina and Algeria, the French waged a classic colonial war, in the sense that their objective was to preserve their colonial sovereignty. The US approach was quite different: they in no way sought to replace the French by becoming the new occupying power. Their aim was neo-colonial rather than colonial, inasmuch as they fought to support the Saigon regime, which, despite being corrupt, brutal, and dictatorial, was nonetheless Vietnamese, and thus national. The United States' political objective was not to control the territory but to maintain a geostrategic advantage.

Once again, these historical developments are reflected with remarkable clarity in the history of aviation. Classic colonial 'police bombing', that of the 1920s and thirties, was marked by a contradiction between the technical means employed and the political ends: whereas aviation already tended to a location beyond sovereignty, classic colonialism continued to seek local appropriation of a territory. Since the United States precisely did not have the objective of appropriating Vietnamese territory, aviation logically became the privileged arm in their war. However, a war beyond a locally anchored sovereignty is ipso facto a war beyond just a state horizon. By all these features, the Vietnam War prefigured the developments of warfare that we see today. A combatant that seeks to avoid ground occupation is naturally led to focus on air power so as to physically eliminate all those who resist.

CHAPTER 10

World Governance and Perpetual War

'Mr President, it's a serious time,' said National Security Adviser Brent Scowcroft, 'Iraq may be about to invade Kuwait.'[1] It was the evening of 1 August 1990, and the last few weeks had been a testing time for President George Bush, who had had to deal simultaneously with an economic crisis and tight budget negotiations with Congress. He thought he deserved a small round of golf to clear his head. But the reaction set in immediately: he felt a bad pain in his shoulders, unaccustomed to the effort of dispatching the equivalent of a bucket's worth of golf balls. Dressed in a T-shirt, sitting legs apart on the examination table, he was given heat treatment and had other worries on his mind than some troop movements on the other side of the world.[2] He dismissed his national security adviser, and only five days later began to understand 'the enormity of Iraq'.[3]

During the month of August 1990, the US administration gradually took stock of the events taking place in Mesopotamia. The world situation was still tense: the people's republics of Eastern Europe had collapsed one after the other, the Berlin Wall had fallen, and Germany would soon be reunited. It was in this month of August, however, that the US administration was faced with the wide range

---

1   George Bush with Brent Scowcroft, *A World Transformed*, New York: Vintage, 1999, 302.

2   Ibid.

3   George Bush, *All the Best, George Bush: My Life in Letters and Other Writings*, New York: Scribner, 1999; entry for 5 August 1990, 476.

of political possibilities opened up by the Iraqi invasion of Kuwait: after the collapse of the Soviet bloc, nothing less than a new global configuration, a 'new world order'. As President Bush noted on 7 September: 'The importance of the United States is brought home to me clearly. It's only the United States that can lead. All countries in the West have to turn to us.'[4]

In many respects, the last decade of the twentieth century was an unprecedented period in geostrategic terms. Between 1989 and 1991, the Soviet Union, the principal 'contender', collapsed without having been defeated in war, along with the people's republics in its zone of influence. If there is nothing abnormal in the disappearance of a contender, the peaceful collapse of a great power is a very unusual case in history. Equally singular is the fact that the early twenty-first century has been marked by the absence of a Hobbesian contender on the international stage. China, undergoing an irresistible rise and presenting all the hallmarks of a Hobbesian regime, is in the process of becoming the main rival power. Yet the military domination of the United States remains historically unprecedented. The US military budget makes up 40 per cent of world military expenditure (a long way ahead of China with 9.5 per cent, Russia's 5.2 per cent, and the UK's 3.5 per cent), so that the monopoly of means of exercising violence on the world scale has probably never been as supreme as it is today. In the face of this crushing superiority, what country would dare defy the military power of the hegemon?

Is it an exaggeration to say that the dream of perpetual peace has never been so close to realization as since the fall of the Soviet Union? The 'new world order' sketched

---

4   Ibid., 479.

out by President Bush in his famous speech pointed decidedly in this direction. Let us return to 11 September 1990.
According to George Bush, Sr, the world of the new era
that was opening would be 'a world where the rule of law
supplants the rule of the jungle. A world in which nations
recognize the shared responsibility for freedom and justice.
A world where the strong respect the rights of the weak'.[5]
This world, which would be 'freer from the threat of terror,
stronger in the pursuit of justice, and more secure in the
quest for peace', fits firmly in the long tradition of cosmopolitism. In concrete terms, it meant that the United States
had to 'defend civilized values around the world and maintain our economic power at home'. This speech, with its
flagrant borrowings from colonial rhetoric, scarcely concealed the geostrategic stake represented by Kuwaiti oil.
The new era, 'in which the nations of the world, East and
West, North and South, can prosper and live in harmony'
was inconceivable without American hegemony. '[T]here
is no substitute for American leadership. In the face of
tyranny, let no one doubt American credibility and reliabil-
ity. Let no one doubt our staying power.' If the armed force
was American, it represented at the same time the interests
of humanity as a whole: the coming war would not just be
'the United States against Iraq. It is Iraq against the world.'
As everyone knows, this speech on the new world order
of peace was the preparation for a war that would make
unprecedented use of air power.

The fall of the Soviet Union was not simply a geopolitical event of first importance, with political consequences
not limited to those countries and regions formerly under
Soviet domination. The centre itself was affected by the

---

5 George H. W. Bush, 'Address before a joint session of Congress,
September 11, 1990', http://millercenter.org/president/bush/speeches/
speech-3425

generalization of the 'rollback agenda', initiated by the election of Margaret Thatcher in 1979 and that of Ronald Reagan in 1980, which consisted in undoing the various 'historical compromises' that had presided over the establishment of the welfare state in a national context. The historical cycle that begun in 1914 was in the process of closing. Old nationalisms, the age of world wars and welfare, the glorious years of the post-war boom, were coming to an end. A new social and political model was being put in place, both nationally and globally. This new situation naturally affected the form taken by conflicts, and the evolution of air warfare provides a good indicator of this.

In the early 1990s, the disappearance of the Soviet contender and the spectre of Communism made it possible to renew the link between economic liberalism and perpetual peace, as in the period before the First World War. After the fall of the Berlin Wall, the object was to destroy, both within states and in the external environment, anything that was capable of obstructing the free circulation of goods and capital, and everything that posed an obstacle to generalized competition. In sum, to pursue, in a context of unipolar hegemony unprecedented on a world scale, a political programme alternately known as 'neoliberalism', 'deregulation', or 'globalization'. This led to a number of consequences at the level of 'international security'.

First of all, the armed forces no more escaped outsourcing and privatization than the rest of the public sector. For example, by the time that the US troops deployed in Iraq were withdrawn in 2010, the number of mercenaries on the ground there was greater than that of regular soldiers.[6] This brought to an end the old form of state

---

6 In a wide-ranging literature devoted to this, see in particular Gerald Schumacher, *A Bloody Business: America's War Zone Contractors and the Occupation of Iraq*, St Paul: Zenith Press, 2006.

power whose ideal-type was the control of physical violence: a military-fiscal state based on the monopolization
of violence – this being itself controlled by the disciplinary
power developed and perfected in the armed forces, whose
counterweight was the state's assumption of responsibility
for the 'social problem'. Neoliberalism, on the other hand,
was characterized by what Deleuze and Guattari call a
generalized decoding,[7] including the decoding of violence.
Paradoxically, even while the state was the main actor
responsible for this situation, it was also the state that was
called on to remedy it, inasmuch as the national and social
state remained the object of a desire for re-territorializa-
tion. In other words, whereas the old Marxist tradition
saw the state and its apparatus of violence as simply an
instrument in the service of the bourgeoisie, this could now
access the means of exercising violence without having to
go via the state, as it was now possible to hire the services
of whole armies through private military companies – a
very profitable market.[8]

Secondly, there has been since the 1990s a new tendency
to political, ideological, and military fragmentation almost
everywhere in the world: especially in Africa, but also on
the European periphery, as in the former Yugoslavia. The
global configuration of the Cold War exerted on extremely
varied local conjunctures a power of axiomization – it
was able to bipolarize different conflicts and establish a
series of dichotomies (right/left, reactionary/progressive,
capitalist/Communist) that have since disappeared. The re-
territorializations are now more fragmented, giving rise to

---

7 Gilles Deleuze and Félix Guattari, *Anti-Oedipus: Capitalism
and Schizophrenia*, London: Penguin, 2009.
8 Xavier Renou et al., *La Privatisation de la violence. Mercenaires
et societies militaires privées au service du marché*, Marseille: Agone,
2005.

all kinds of 'neo-archaisms', which combine, among other things, identity claims, the invention of new traditionalisms (often religious), the formation of armed gangs prepared to take power and frequently financed by organized crime.

Finally, it is completely logical that this situation, marked by the fragmentation and reconfiguration of state power, calls for a new instance of overcoding: a body not only global but cosmopolitical, which can dichotomize the various local confrontations. That is precisely the function that the 'new world order' is supposed to fulfil. In reality, there is nothing very new about this order, which directly continues forms previously presented as hegemonic cosmopolitism. As might be expected, military aviation is the favoured instrument of this new cosmopolitism, reactivating an imaginary and a system of governance that are already old. We can say, schematically, that the aviation of the hegemonic power takes two major forms: that of an imperial neo-Douhetism, on the one hand, and of a system of 'perpetual low-intensity conflict' on the other. If the Iraq Wars of 1991 and 2003, the Kosovo War of 1999, and that in Libya in 2011 are examples of imperial neo-Douhetism, the massive resort to 'elimination' by drones is the most characteristic feature of this perpetual conflict, directly inherited from colonial warfare.

The leading theorist of this imperial neo-Douhetism is undoubtedly John Warden, whose book *The Air Campaign* was rapidly established as a textbook for the USAF.[9] Warden, a Vietnam veteran, was the architect of the air campaign against Iraq in 1991.[10] The name given to this campaign, 'Instant Thunder', is doubly significant, as it

---

9   John Warden III, *The Air Campaign: Planning for Combat*, Washington, DC: Brassey's Inc., 1989.

10 John Andreas Olsen, *John Warden and the Renaissance of American Air Power*, Washington, DC: Potomac Books, 2007.

recalls the name of a campaign waged in Vietnam, 'Rolling Thunder', despite its differences from this. In North Vietnam, the US Air Force followed the logic of 'coercion', which consisted in making clear to the enemy that, if they did not give in, it would be capable of inflicting still greater damage. For this reason, the intensity of bombing deliberately remained short of what was militarily possible. In 1991, on the contrary, the point was to deploy an 'overwhelming force' that would immediately break any resistance. Instead of 'rolling', the thunder would simply destroy. The enemy was to be paralysed and made incapable of reaction by dealing them a blow of maximal violence. The name given to this air campaign is also significant because it refers exclusively to the strategic bombing of the Democratic Republic of Vietnam; in other words, the massive use of the US Air Force against the guerrilla in the south of the country was passed over in silence, indicating a repression of this traumatic experience that was a widespread phenomenon among the neo-Douhetians. In fact, 'counter-insurrectionary war' is largely absent from their theoretical framework, an absence that John Warden completely accepts: 'Air is of marginal value in a fight against self-sustaining guerrillas, who merge with the population. In this case, no significant target exists for air attack'[11]

As a theorist of 'overwhelming force', Warden remains strongly influenced by Gulio Douhet:

> Central to our thesis is the idea that air superiority is crucial, that a campaign will be lost if the enemy has it, that in many circumstances it alone can win a war, and that its possession is needed before other actions on the ground or in the air can be undertaken.[12]

---

11 Warden, *The Air Campaign*, 125.
12 Ibid., 141.

'Air superiority' – what Douhet called 'command of the air' – was not simply the preliminary to any military action, it could even replace ground action and realize the old dream of controlling a territory without even having to set foot on it. This idea – the basis of British 'air control' in the 1920s and thirties – was reactivated, in the same Iraqi theatre, in the first war under the new world order.

Just like Douhet, Warden believes that the air arm has de facto invalidated the Clausewitzian principle that defence was more economic than attack: contrary to ground weapons, aviation only deployed its true power in the offensive. Like Douhet, he stresses numerical superiority, and prefers missions of 'interdiction' to those of 'close support'. And finally, like Douhet, he relativizes the importance of the ground in favour of the skies: 'Territory may well be the political objective of the campaign, but it rarely should be the military objective.'[13]

Warden's innovation consists in his targeting doctrine. While the Italian theorist is generally associated with the 'terror' bombing of civilian populations, he in fact left the question of targets explicitly open:

> Objectives vary considerably in war, and the choice of them depends chiefly upon the aim sought, whether the command of the air, paralysing the enemy's army and navy, or shattering the morale of civilians behind the lines. This choice may therefore be guided by a great many considerations – military, political, social, and psychological.[14]

Warden proves less flexible than Douhet as far as targeting is concerned: he places targets in a pattern made

---

13   Ibid., 148.
14   Giulio Douhet, *The Command of the Air*, London: Faber and Faber, 1943, 50.

up of five concentric circles. The most important target is the supreme political command. Next come the essential organs of government and command. In third and fourth place we respectively find 'infrastructure' and 'the population'. And at the bottom of the list stands the last objective, the least rewarding one of an air campaign: the enemy's armed forces.[15] It is quite remarkable how, in Warden's schema, population trumps armed forces. As a result, his theory remains in thrall to twentieth-century Douhetism, which, contrary to the classical European theory of war, holds that organized forces are not the central objective of military action.

The USAF colonel John Boyd is another representative of neo-Douhetian thought.[16] Despite not having ever systematized his ideas in a book – his magnum opus, titled *Patterns of Conflict* (1986), is no more than a series of typed notes for a live presentation – his reflections exerted a considerable influence on the United States' strategic reorientation after the Vietnam War.[17] Here the innovation in respect to classical Douhetism is located at two distinct levels: in the conceptualization of the enemy as a 'system', and in 'paralysis' as strategic objective.

---

15   See on this subject John Warden, 'The Enemy as System', *Airpower Journal*, 9 (spring 1995), 40–55: http://ciar.org/ttk/mbt/strategy. Warden.enemy-as-a-system.html

16   Among the wide literature on Boyd, see in particular Joseph Henrotin, *L'Airpower au 21ème siècle: enjeux et perspectives de la stratégie aérienne*, Brussels: Bruylant, 2005.

17   See the argument of Colonel Marshall L. Michel III, *The Revolt of the Majors: How the Air Force Changed after Vietnam*, Auburn University, 2006: https://etd.auburn.edu//handle/10415/595; *Patterns of Conflict* can be found at: http://www.ausairpower.net/JRB/poc.pdf. Another text by Boyd that is often quoted is a short essay, 'Destruction and Creation', which does not directly refer to military strategy (http://www.goalsys.com/books/documents/DESTRUCTION_AND_CREATION.pdf). Both accessed 9 August 2013.

Just like Warden, Boyd presents the enemy not as a single body – whether a government, a command, a leader, and so on – but as a plural and complex system.[18] This change is of great importance, since, as we shall see, it begins a strategic shift that has continued until the present day. Representation of the enemy as a 'system' makes it possible, in particular, to circumvent certain theoretical difficulties that twentieth-century bombing came up against: if the object of bombing was the sovereign people, then the people, at least in Europe, have always been conceived with reference to a state, as the form of its political organization. It is the state, in the last instance, that takes the decision to capitulate. The critique that Foucault addressed to political thought applies just as much to strategic thought: 'We still have not cut off the head of the king'.[19]

The second conceptual innovation of neo-Douhetism, strategic paralysis as the objective of an air campaign, is based on two historical references: the lessons of the Marxist revolutionary guerrilla and the German doctrine of blitzkrieg. According to Boyd, every complex system has to endow itself with a subsystem that he calls OODA (Observation—Orientation—Decision—Action) in order to interact with its environment. Initially developed with a view to aerial combat, but quickly adapted to all levels of warfare and every kind of confrontation, the theory of the 'OODA loop' called for the interruption of the operation of this subsystem: to disturb observation, confuse orientation, and prevent decisions being taken, in order to reduce the system to inaction and thus paralyse it. The objective of paralysis makes it possible to

---

18 David S. Fadok, *John Boyd and John Warden: Air Power's Quest for Strategic Paralysis*, The War College Series, n.d.

19 Michel Foucault, *A History of Sexuality, Volume 1: An Introduction*, New York: Vintage, 1990, 88–9.

bipass a practical, political, and moral difficulty of classical bombing, since it is no longer necessary to target the people. Neo-Douhetism thus permits, in theory, a renewal of the principle of immunity of civilian populations, even if in practice, as we shall see, things do not always go so well.

These two key points of neo-Douhetism – the enemy as complex system and paralysis as the objective – enable certain inherent difficulties of classic Douhetism to be overcome: the conception of the enemy as system makes it possible to dispense with the monarchical representation of politics, and the objective of paralysis makes it no longer necessary to target the people directly. But the second innovation tends to negate the theoretical advantages of the first, since the system that neo-Douhetism seeks to paralyse remains a state. It is rather the second contemporary approach in air war, 'perpetual low-intensity war', that represents an advance from this point of view.

Let us, however, examine first of all what an air campaign of the neo-Douhetian type resembles in practice. Take for example the ideal-type campaign: operation 'Desert Storm' conducted against Iraq in 1991. The battle for 'command of the air' comes first, both logically and chronologically. Every operation has first of all to neutralize enemy anti-aircraft defence systems. Given the unmatched superiority of US forces, this first level has not posed any serious problem, either in Iraq or elsewhere. The air campaign goes on to follow the hierarchy of objectives laid down by Warden: the supreme command, the 'essential organs' of government and command, infrastructure, the population, and finally the armed forces. The objective, once command of the air is obtained, is thus to 'decapitate' the enemy social system. But it is here that things get more complicated. As everyone knows, Saddam Hussein was not killed by bombs from the air (any more than were Slobodan Milosevic or Muammar Gaddafi), a fact that demonstrates the difficulty of striking the supreme political command. The vital organs of government and command may well be more numerous and easier to reach, but it would be an exaggeration to claim that they ceased to function in the Iraqi case. There remains, therefore, in decreasing order of importance, the population and the armed forces.

Neo-Douhetian bombing campaigns only target populations indirectly, by way of infrastructure. Since the disaster of the Vietnam War, a disaster particularly in terms of the image of the United States in the world, the military doctrines of the Western powers advocate respect for civilians and reassert the classic principle of proportionality, according to which the damage inflicted on a population should not exceed the military advantages brought by the bombing. And yet, in practice, the 'indirect' effects of an attack can prove just as disastrous as its direct ones. Still worse, it is not even necessary to use military means to decimate a population. To persist with the Iraqi example, the 'economic sanctions' that followed the war of 1990–91 had such an impact on the civilian population that Denis Halliday, humanitarian coordinator of the United Nations in Baghdad, declared that he would refuse to administer such a 'genocidal' programme. It goes without saying that the results of such a blockade bear hardest on the most vulnerable – children, the sick, the elderly, the poor. Confronted with the fact that the sanctions against Iraq had caused the deaths of half a million children – more than twice the number of victims of the attacks on Hiroshima and Nagasaki combined – Madeleine Albright, United States secretary of state, replied: 'I think this is a very hard choice, but the price – we think the price is worth it.'[20]

Bombing can sometimes have just as dramatic 'indirect effects'. In January 1991, ten days after the start of operation 'Desert Storm', more than 75 per cent of the Iraq electricity network was destroyed and the water supply completely stopped functioning in the centre and south of the country.[21] The effects of a prolonged blackout are beyond understanding: according to a report published by the German Bundestag, a blackout of more than two weeks would inevitably lead to 'a collapse of the whole society'.[22] The operational implementation of imperial neo-Douhetism thus does indeed target the civilian population – but indirectly, by way of the systematic destruction of infrastructure.

The Iraqi campaign of 1991 had a further characteristic. By dint of their crushing superiority, the Americans could afford the luxury of waging two air campaigns at the same time, attacking not only the command centres and infrastructure, as recommended by Warden and Boyd, but also, quite simply, the Iraqi army itself: they waged a classic campaign in parallel with a neo-Douhetian campaign that aimed to paralyse the enemy system. As the commander of operations was an army general, a certain rivalry between the services was probably a further factor, as well as the desire to seriously diminish Iraqi military capacity.

---

20 Adam Jones, *Genocide: A Comprehensive Introduction*, London: Routledge, 2010, 45.

21 Robert A. Pape, *Bombing to Win: Air Power and Coercion in War*, Ithaca: Cornell University Press, 1996, 228–9.

22 Thomas Petermann, Harald Bradke, Arne Lüllmann, Maik Poetzsch, and Ulrich Riehm, *Gefährdung und Verletzbarkeit moderner Gesellschaften – am Beispiel eines grossräumigen Ausfalls der Stromversorgung*, Büro für Technikfolgen-abschätzung beim Deutschen Bundestag, November 2010, 3.

How was the war envisaged from the Iraqi side? Saddam Hussein was sufficiently realistic not to count on victory on the battlefield. His strategy, at the level of politics rather than the strictly military, rested on the 'casualty aversion' that many analysts have detected to be a concern of American society since the Vietnam War. Making a calculation that seemed anything but unreasonable, he estimated that his army – 300,000 men, 3,500 tanks, and 2,500 artillery pieces – was capable of inflicting on the enemy losses of around 10,000 men, which would be sufficient to make them leave the country. The reality would prove this to be sadly mistaken: only 148 US soldiers died in combat, including thirty-five victims of 'friendly fire'.[23] The Iraqi army was far from negligible in number, yet it did not stand a chance. During the 1990s and early 2000s the conviction developed on the US side that war was at an end: what adversary would be so stupid as to think they could resist such a fearsome force?[24] The capacity for military projection seemed no longer limited, to the point that the hegemonic power dreamed of steadily invading all the countries it had problems with to establish regimes more in line with its interests. According to General Wesley Clark, in November 2001 the Pentagon drew up a five-year plan designed to successively overthrow the regimes in Iraq, Syria, Lebanon, Libya, Iran, Somalia, and Sudan.[25] Rather than 'real wars', these operations were supposed to be short-term operations, as no force would be able to resist the overwhelming superiority of the United States.

---

23   In addition to the combat fatalities, an almost equal number of 145 died in accidents that were not directly linked to combat.

24   See David Kilcullen, *The Accidental Guerrilla: Fighting Small Wars in the Midst of a Big One*, London: Hurst, 2009, 1.

25   Wesley K. Clark, *Winning Modern Wars: Iraq, Terrorism, and the American Empire*, New York: Public Affairs, 2003, 130.

This superiority was also based on informational control of the battlefield. Since 1996, the concept of 'full spectrum dominance' has been fully integrated into American military doctrine.[26] This refers not only to command of the field of physical confrontation – whether on land, sea, or air – but also to command of the radio spectrum, information, and cyberspace, though this poses a far from negligible challenge in terms of information processing, running the risk of a paralysing 'information overload'. Thus, a significant current in US military debate from the 1990s on has studied the implications of 'network-centric warfare'.[27] Thanks to its military, technical, and financial superiority, the United States was capable of defeating any enemy on the planet. Still better, according to the 'two war strategy', the overwhelming force deployed in a rerun blitzkrieg would even permit the hegemon to crush two adversaries at the same time. Once the hostile government was defeated, US troops would leave the territory to focus on new tasks. A new government would then exercise democratic sovereignty, open its frontiers to foreign capital, and align itself to the rules of economic liberalism. The 'new world order' that George W. Bush prepared to impose in 2001, following ideas sketched ten years earlier by his father, was thus conceived as an international system based on sovereign capitalist states and stabilized by the American hegemonic centre. His interventions, powerful yet brief, aimed to ensure political homogeneity on the world scale, and to make all states adopt the

---

26 Joint Chiefs of Staff, *Joint Vision 2010, America's Military Preparing for Tomorrow* (http://www.dtic.mil/jv2010/jv2010.pdf, 26–27, accessed 10 August 2013).

27 David S. Alberts, John J. Garstka, Richard E. Hayes, and David S. Signori, *Understanding Information Age Warfare*, CCRA Publications, 2001.

model of a representative democracy committed to liberal capitalism.

As everyone knows, the Bush family's plan failed, for various reasons that bear on the logic of the world system as well as on strictly strategic logic. The capitalist world system inevitably produces imbalances, zones of 'underdevelopment', 'neo-archaisms', spatial and temporal incommensurabilities, which makes it impossible to conceive 'globalization' as a one-dimensional process of homogenization or convergence of social or political models. The attempts that aimed to impose a 'new world order', however, based on brief interventions designed to establish 'democratic' regimes and conducted with the 'overwhelming force' of neo-Douhetian air campaigns, believed precisely in this convergence. In other words, the desired result could be assumed in advance. By representing the enemy as homogeneous to oneself, this gave rise to an unpardonable error at the military level, characteristic of all forms of Douhetism: failure to recognize the fundamental characteristic of war, that of being an antagonistic relationship. On this basis, the neo-Douhetian interventions even helped to consolidate the enemy, against whom all their overwhelming force ultimately proved impotent. The Iraqi example remains a paradigm in this respect: by targeting the apparatuses of the enemy state, neo-Douhetism itself created the conditions for a 'war machine', a non-state body, to turn against states, including the one that conducted the intervention.

If it is therefore foolish to believe that American force can be resisted on a classic battlefield, an intelligent adversary will naturally opt for a different terrain and a different type of combat. He will take the war onto a terrain where 'overwhelming force' will be likely to prove ineffective. Such an adversary will not wage a classic type of war, but a guerrilla combined with terrorist acts to bring the war 'amongst the population'.[28] This is precisely what happened in the wake of the attacks of 11 September 2001 and the invasions of Afghanistan and Iraq. And this brings us to 'perpetual low-intensity war'.

'Total wars' that involve one or more contenders, and 'asymmetrical' wars against insurgents and guerrillas, have one thing in common: in both cases, the great power is led to strike hard in order to win rapidly. This was the approach in both world conflicts, and it was also the approach of the United States in Vietnam. In the case of asymmetrical conflicts of the colonial and neo-colonial type, time works inevitably in favour of the insurgents, and the great power loses as long as it does not win.[29] According to the Israeli military theorist Martin van Creveld, there are only two ways of defeating an insurrection, the first illustrated by the British approach in Northern Ireland, and the second by that of the Syrian state against the Muslim Brotherhood insurrection of 1982.[30] The British success in Northern Ireland was due to the quality of their intelligence services, the good training of their troops, and the political decision to limit the number of victims as far as possible, so as not to alienate the civilian population. The Syrian strategy of 1982 was precisely the opposite: instead of showing discernment, the state decided to strike a single great blow of unprecedented violence. The bombing of the city of Hama brought the deaths of between 10,000 and 40,000 civilians – and the insurrection was snuffed out.

---

28 For the concept of 'war amongst the people', see Rupert Smith, *The Utility of Force: The Art of War in the Modern World*, London: Allen Lane, 2005.

29 Martin van Creveld, *The Changing Face of War: Combat from the Marne to Iraq, 2008*, New York: Ballantine, 2008, 219–29.

30 Ibid., 229–46.

A democratic country such as the United States is by nature very poorly placed to defeat an insurrection. The war in Vietnam showed the key importance of public opinion: when this turned against the war, the insurgents gained a decisive advantage. This turn was all the more likely, in that the country where the United States was waging war was far from its own territory and the nation's vital interests were not at stake. Why then, the question became, go on fighting on the other side of the world, in countries that we do not understand and where we are not loved? The 'new counter-insurrectionary strategy' of the US Air Force sought precisely to secure this open flank, by changing the very context of the struggle. Counter-insurrectionary actions would be conducted, but care would be taken not to cross the threshold beyond which public opinion would perceive the conflict as a 'war'. In other words, the actions could be intrinsically quite close to classic doctrines of counter-insurrection; what changes is the fact that they take place outside the context that has traditionally defined war. The majority of counter-insurrectionary air actions are now conducted in regions that are officially 'at peace'. The new approach thus implies a deliberate blurring of the border dividing war from peace; it is even tempting to say that imperial perpetual peace now coincides with a perpetual low-intensity war.

The most obvious example is provided once again by air war, and more precisely, by the massive use of drones, particularly in such countries as Pakistan and Yemen. In reality, the blurring of borders between war and peace goes far beyond these new devices. As we have seen, it was already embryonic in the first air strikes, inasmuch as these were not directed against armed forces, but against political and socio-economic systems. The roots of this blurring can also be found in total wars, where economic systems;

infrastructure; and the political, social, and 'moral' coherence of peoples become not only targets but also, by the same token, moral stakes to defend, military assets to fortify, political bases to establish. The very notion of 'total war' implies that the military and civilian domains are no longer seen as staunchly separated. And finally, the same roots can be found in colonial wars, in particular in the practice of 'police bombing', such that Negri and Hardt are found to write that today, perpetual low-intensity war merges together with high-intensity global police operations.[31]

To locate contemporary global violence in the same genealogical lineage as total (especially European) war and colonial war clearly does not amount to maintaining that there is nothing new under the sun. On the contrary, this approach makes us attentive to significant moments of rupture. Thus, if it is true that the 'people', organized 'democratically', constitute the primary object of classic strategic bombing, it is worth inquiring what concepts of people and democracy the new forms of violence correspond to.

The contemporary muddying of borders between war and peace is openly proclaimed in military doctrines developed since the 1990s, those of the United States in particular. Of clearly neo-Douhetian inspiration, the concept of 'shock and awe' emphasized the necessity to counter any attempt to take the conflict outside the limits of conventional war.[32] The concept of 'full spectrum dominance'

---

31 Michael Hardt and Antonio Negri, *Multitude: War and Democracy in the Age of Empire*, London: Penguin, 2005, 22.

32 Harlan K. Ullman and James P. Wade (with L. A. 'Bud' Edney, Fred M. Franks, Charles A. Horner, Jonathan T. Howe, and Keith Brendley), *Shock and Awe: Achieving Rapid Dominance*, National Defence University, 1996, available at http://www.dodccrp.org/files/Ullman_Shock.pdf, accessed 11 August 2013.

emphasizes the need to dominate all spaces in which confrontation might erupt, especially 'in situations where we cannot bring our technological capabilities fully to bear against opponents who seek to nullify our technological superiority by various means'.[33] The concepts of 'effects-based operations' and 'fourth-generation warfare' go still more clearly in this direction, in that they explicitly employ 'non-military' methods to attain objectives that are indistinctly military and civil.[34] The same holds for the Chinese concept of 'unrestricted warfare'.

What we see here is a radicalization of total military mobilization, to the point that it becomes impossible to distinguish what is military and what is not. If the realm of the military obviously includes, on top of conventional military action, guerrilla war and terrorism, it now extends to economics, law, the media, and culture. The Chinese strategists Qiao Liang and Wang Xiangsui, for example, have developed the scenario of an attack that would consist first of all in provoking a financial crisis in the enemy nation, by way of stock market speculation, then in using computer viruses to attack the electricity network, the media, telecommunications, and air traffic control. This would almost automatically create a situation of panic, contestation, and sociopolitical crisis. Physical violence would be only the last stage in this 'unrestricted warfare'.[35]

The wars of the future will be long, even interminable, decentred and lacking a national basis. They will potentially involve the whole of the world population. The combatants themselves will no longer belong to military

33 *Joint Vision 2010*, 27, accessed 11 August 2013.

34 Thomas X. Hammes, *The Sling and the Stone: On War in the 21st Century*, St. Paul: Zenith Press, 2006.

35 Qiao Liang and Wang Xiangsui, *Unrestricted Warfare: China's Master Plan to Destroy America*, Los Angeles: Pan American Publishing Company, 2002.

apparatuses, but to decentralized groups, often ephemeral, and endowed with variable hierarchies. In sum, this means reckoning with networks that are capable of coagulating locally and temporarily to form fighting nuclei, rather than pyramidal institutions with a monopoly of violence.

If this description closely resembles the paranoiac fantasy of an ungraspable enemy characteristic of colonial and neo-colonial wars, its 'Orientalist' stereotype now serves as a model for the imperial forces. The neo-Douhetian John Boyd thus insists in *Patterns of Conflict* that it is absolutely necessary to decentralize command structures. He draws here on the German concept of 'mission-type tactics' (*Auftragstaktik*), in which the superior officer defines a mission to be accomplished, sets a precise date, and allocates the forces available, but leaves to his subordinates the task of finding the means to realize the mission.[36] This devolution offers an adaptive capacity that is greater, more effective, and quicker than a classic chain of command. The risk is clearly that the various decentralized actions lose their strategic coherence. But long years of training will develop in all agents a similar view of the world and an unshakeable belief in the justice of the cause for which they are fighting.[37] These 'flat hierarchies' and network military organization are clearly inspired not just by certain groups of terrorists and insurgents, but also by new managerial approaches and what is commonly called 'post-Fordism'. In this expanded context of 'perpetual low-intensity war', aviation is entrusted with a role palpably different from that which it plays in the imperial neo-Douhetian system.

36 The classic formulation of this concept of '*innere Führung*' is found in Wolf Graf Baudissin, *Soldat für den Frieden. Entwürfe für eine zeitgemässe Bundeswehr*, Munich: Piper, 1970, 117–33.

37 Boyd, 'Patterns of Conflict', especially 72, 74, 143, and 144.

Drones, remotely guided and without a crew, are the most striking illustration of this new role.[38] Developed first of all for reconnaissance and surveillance missions, they are increasingly equipped with bombs and missiles. They thus serve at the same time to monitor, locate, and destroy. Since the election of Barack Obama, US drones have carried out an ever-growing number of strikes, particularly in Pakistan, but also in Yemen and Somalia. Extremely powerful video cameras enable these devices to register the movements of 'suspects', usually intermediate cadres of terrorist networks, to follow their movements and then eliminate them. As for the designation of targets, this is carried out in two different modalities. At a weekly briefing at the White House, known as 'bloody Thursday', the president personally approves the list of people to kill in the coming week. Alongside these 'personality strikes' there are 'signature strikes', which, as distinct from the former, do not target known individuals but persons presenting a 'suspect' behaviour. On 14 January 2010, for example, seventeen men were killed by a drone in Pakistan because they had been seen training, drilling, and running close to a Taliban camp.[39]

The use of drones is also a continuation of various twentieth-century genealogies of war. The drone clearly assumes the colonial practice of 'police bombing', in the sense that in both cases air bombing takes place in time of 'peace'. The colonial control of the 1920s and thirties likewise prefigured low-intensity air war, inasmuch as bombing was combined with a surveillance mission. While the ground approaches of colonial war counted on criss-crossing the territory, 'police bombing' promised to realize a complete

---

38   See in particular the particularly interesting book by Grégoire Chamayou, *A Theory of the Drone*, New York: The New Press, 2015.
39   *Washington Post*, 23 October 2013.

control by panoptic vision: surveillance by overflying. What was no more than a dream in the 1920s and thirties is now becoming possible. The cameras fitted to drones are capable of recording every movement in a given region, permitting analysts to go back in time to know what a suspect was doing at a given moment, where he was coming from, and where he was going. Surveillance is in the process of becoming total.

From this point of view, and taking into account the extension of the notion of war to every field of human activity, generalized computer surveillance by intelligence services clearly runs in the same direction. Drones are most commonly employed not for bombing but for surveillance missions. Besides, they are used above all not by the US army but by the secret services, even for bombing missions, which well shows that surveillance and elimination are two poles of a single continuum. The drone also fits into another tradition of counter-insurrectionary war, which counts primarily on intelligence so as to limit physical confrontation as far as possible, and thus also the number of victims. Contrary to colonial and neo-colonial conflicts, the physical elimination of the largest possible number of insurgents, real or presumed, is no longer the proclaimed objective. This explains why the numbers killed by drones are much lower than the number of victims that a large-scale conflict would produce. To remain with the example of the drones used in Pakistan, it is estimated that the various US services conduct an average of one strike every four days, and that up to this point they have killed a minimum of 2,562 persons, or more likely 3,300. Among these victims were between 474 and 881 civilians, including 176 children.[40]

---

40 International Human Rights and Conflict Resolution Clinic at Stanford Law School and Global Justice Clinic at NYU School of Law,

The strategic emphasis placed on total surveillance and limiting the number of victims does not mean that the administration of physical death is no longer on the agenda, simply that the representation of the enemy has changed – a change that we can assess by comparison with the approach of the United States to Vietnam. The Viet Cong, imagined as omnipresent, actually had forms of organization that were reducible in principle to tree diagrams: a hierarchical and pyramidal structure based on a differentiation of functions and guided by an enlightened 'vanguard'. Tactically, the US objective was to rise up the hierarchical chain, decapitation being simply the final stage in the physical elimination of all insurgents at every level. Today, on the other hand, insurgents are no longer represented as tree structures but as 'networks'. A network, for its part, is organized around strategic 'nodes' that give it temporary stability. As well as conducting total surveillance, today's counter-insurrectionary strategy consists in attacking and eliminating these nodes, in the hope of causing the network to disintegrate. The intermediate cadres of terrorist networks, who are the targets of drone strikes, precisely constitute nodes of this kind, and according to the champions of remote-control warfare, their elimination necessarily leads to the disintegration of the network. As might be expected, events develop differently in reality, and all the available evidence gives us to believe that these 'nodes' immediately regroup, in the manner of the heads of the hydra.

A certain number of conclusions can be drawn from the evolution of military and policing doctrines and practices.

Living Under Drones: Death, Injury, and Trauma to Civilians From US Drone Practices in Pakistan, (2012), http://livingunderdrones. http://www.chrgj.org/wp-content/uploads/2012/10/Living-Under-Drones.pdf, 45.

The stages of air war in the twentieth century, as we have seen, coincided with changes in 'democracy' and the 'people'. How does this relate to air war today? It is relatively easy to answer this question as far as imperial neo-Douhetism is concerned. The Douhetians seek to paralyse a political system strategically in order to provoke a change of government or even of regime. Like their predecessors in this tradition, they never clearly explain how this change is expected to happen, if not by a coup d'état or revolution. The agents of change are thus either factions of the elite (for a coup d'état) or the mass of the people (in the case of a revolution). A change of regime by coup d'état seems to be envisaged particularly for 'tribal' societies such as Iraq or Libya, countries where the state appears as an entity negotiated between different chiefs. In this first case, the theoretical foundation is thus exactly the same as that of the police bombing practised in the inter-war years. In the second case, it is exactly that which formed the basis of the old Douhetian tradition: politics is based ultimately on the 'people', a people whose nature is not defined, nor, in all likelihood, can it be. In sum, neo-Douhetism rests on the same hypotheses as the two versions of classic air war: the Douhetism of total war, and colonial police bombing.

The true novelty, therefore, does not lie in neo-Douhetism itself, but in the perpetual low-intensity air war exemplified by the use of hunter-killer drones. Contrary to what might be believed, the main advantage of these devices is not really that they bestow an invulnerability on the side using them. To understand this, one need only consider the losses in the last neo-Douhetian air campaigns. A joke circulating in aviation circles suggests that it is safer to fly in a war zone than in a zone of peace. Even against an army as formidable as the Iraqi army in 1991, the Americans lost only 148 men in combat. In regions such as Pakistan or Yemen, and against adversaries lacking anti-aircraft defence, the losses in materiel and personnel are negligible or even non-existent.

A further advantage, more directly political, seems far more important. The drone bombers bring a technical solution to the problem posed by operations that can essentially be characterized as 'policing' but which are conducted with military intensity and on a world scale. Drones are, so to say, the complement of force to what Jürgen Habermas calls 'global domestic policy' (*Weltinnenpolitik*). They are the deadly truncheon of the global cop. Concretely, this role is assumed today by a great democratic power, the United States. Yet the manner in which this state conducts its military operations inevitably has a feedback effect on the functioning of its institutions and its politics in general.

It is highly significant from this point of view that the majority of drones are piloted not by the US Army but by the CIA, in other words, the secret services, which by definition escape the control of democratic public opinion. They are the weapon of choice for the 'post-heroic war' championed by the strategist Edward Luttwak,[41] a war that spares the problem of mobilization and, by the same token, any democratic debate on the desirability of war, which remains, despite everything, an extraordinary and exceptional event in the life of a nation. They are the arm of a war that is no longer a war but a police operation, and which thus does not pertain to foreign policy but to current affairs and the *arcana imperii*. In sum, a war deprived of that 'democratic' potential which is *also* part of the legacy of the great butcheries of the nineteenth and twentieth centuries. From this point of view, the use of bomber drones for global police functions is directly bound up with a

---

41 Edward Luttwak, 'Toward Post-Heroic Warfare', *Foreign Affairs*, 74/3 (May–June 1995), 109–22.

tendency that is intrinsic to modern democracy yet largely repressed: its 'totalitarian' tendency.⁴²

All the same, the totalitarianism of war by drones differs in many respects from that of the wars of the twentieth century. The fundamental difference lies in the fact that these historical totalitarianisms, whether of the fascist or Stalinist type, were always based on the 'people'. There exists, from this point of view, 'an inner solidarity between democracy and totalitarianism',⁴³ even if, as distinct from democratic regimes, totalitarianisms constructed this 'people' according to a primary vector to which they subordinated all others: either class or the racialized nation. At all events, this 'people', the principal entity of politics, also became the principal target. In the great conflicts of the twentieth century, the people were taken as target in order to unmake their unity and transform them into their opposite, the populace. Conversely, a whole series of nationalized social policies aimed to strengthen their unity.

It is from this point of view that perpetual low-intensity war marks a particularly important break. Imperial neo-Douhetism remains in the lineage of total war inasmuch as it aims to defeat a state, by impelling the people to rise against it. Perpetual low-intensity war, on the other hand, is directly linked to a global war machine that goes beyond states. It attacks territories placed under the sovereignty of

---

42 'Totalitarian' in Giorgio Agamben's sense. Cf. *Homo Sacer*, Stanford: Stanford University Press, 1988, 10, as well as Gilles Deleuze and Félix Guattari, *A Thousand Plateaus: Capitalism and Schizophrenia*, Minneapolis: University of Minnesota Press, 1987, especially 434. As far as US policy in particular is concerned, this tendency is exemplified by the temptation of the 'imperial presidency' that has been detectable since the time of the Vietnam War. See the classic work by Arthur Meier Schlesinger Jr, *The Imperial Presidency*, Mariner Books, 2004.

43 Agamben, *Homo Sacer*, 10.

post-colonial states, thus subordinating their sovereignty to its global logic. In fact, it is even improper to say that this perpetual war attacks 'territories', precisely because, coming from above, it is by its essence de-territorialized.

Targets today are no longer 'peoples', but strategic nodes inscribed in networks. If the bombed peoples of the twentieth century were eminently nationalized entities, today's networks are cosmopolitan, with flows that cross borders. They are transnational and even global. As a result, perpetual low-intensity war itself becomes globalized. From this point of view, colonial police bombing may well form the historical matrix of the wars of the future. History is already being repeated: low-intensity air war is waged in the same theatres as the police bombing of the inter-war years. Will history also be repeated on another level, by submitting the whole world population to such practices in a few years from now?

It is impossible to say. But, according to the logic of perpetual low-intensity war, today's aerial bombing is simply one pole in a global counter-insurrection strategy, the other pole of which is total surveillance. What we can say with certainty is that this surveillance already extends to the entire world population.

Index

Index

Index

Index